I'm grateful that you're reading my book.
I hope that your life is full of blessings.
Sincerely,
Sally K. Browne

Grateful and Blessed

Thanks to Family, Friends, and Strangers

SALLY K. BROWNE

ISBN–978-0-578-33278-9

Dedication

To Dave, Michael, Kathleen, and Aaliya

Acknowledgements

A ginormous thank you to my brother-in-law, John Browne, for once again turning my written words into a book, and to my daughter, Kathleen, for always saying "Sure" whenever I asked for her help in this process.

Joe Burbank, thank you for quickly saying "Yes" when I asked if you would design the cover.

I'm also sincerely grateful to Father Charlie Mitchell for writing the beautiful Foreword to my book, and to Brendan Linnane, attorney extraordinaire, for answering my many legal questions.

Most of all, heartfelt gratitude for my husband, Dave, for all his love and support throughout the years, and for a lifetime of adventures. He's the reason why my life's gratitude list is so long.

Foreword

As we enter the new year, I find the idea of a "gratitude journal" timely. The collective weariness we have all felt in this era of Covid has had such a darkening effect on our souls, pulling us into the shades of fear and pushing us away from our sources of support and strength.

And yet the blessings of our lives have still found their way in, maybe in ways unexpected, which makes the experience so much the better. This wonderful journal of gratitude composed by Sally Browne is evidence of just that.

I have known Sally and her family going on thirty years. As pastor of her parish, I have seen her son and daughter grow in wisdom and grace, I have witnessed the joys and sorrows of her family, with the long suffering of her dear mother with dementia, and Sally's extraordinary effort to bring comfort, dignity and love to her Mom and her aunt as they approached death. There was also the heartbreak of her husband Dave's untimely death. And yet, as you will read in these pages, there have been so many occasions of blessing, and of Sally's response – one of gratitude.

St. Paul in his letter to the Colossians says this: "...let the peace of Christ rule in your hearts, to which indeed you were called in the one body. And be grateful. Let the word of Christ dwell in you richly...." Pope Francis writes: "Gratitude makes the world better, transmits hope."

That, I think is what this work of Sally's accomplishes – transmitting hope. And we need that, for without hope there is, frankly, no life.

Sally has opened her heart and given us entry into her daily doings, shining on those daily events we all share the light of gratitude. In doing so she has given us the means to bring that same light to the events of our own lives, and to color them with gratitude.

I hope you take inspiration from this work, and maybe pick up a pen and begin to record your own journal of gratitude.

Rev. Charles Mitchell, Pastor
St. Mary Magdalen Catholic Church

Preface

I have so much in my life to be grateful for—my children, my good health, a wonderful family, friends who are like family, a country where I can practice my religion, a fulfilling career, and decades with my husband who was the love of my life, and who was smitten with me.

Those are the most important things in my life. There is no need to write them down so that I can remember them. That's because they are close to my heart and I thank God for them every day of my life. I could never forget any of them. However, over the past few years I started thinking about a gratitude journal to help me remember the happy details of my daily life that I often forget ever happened.

I will always remember that my son got married two years ago. I will always be grateful that he found the love of his life. However, I honestly can't remember most of the small things that happened two years ago that brightened my days, that made me smile, and that helped me when I needed help. It's not that I didn't appreciate those things when they happened. It's that there is so much that happens every day in each of our lives, that it would be impossible to remember all the joy, and happiness, and sighs of relief that we experience.

That is the reason I thought that it would be a good idea to keep a gratitude journal. I want to be able to remember all the things that I'm grateful for each and every day. I want to be able to read my journal when the year is drawing to a close and celebrate what a great year I had.

In recent years I started the New Year by writing in my journal each day, but I found it to be hard work, and my stick-to-itiveness left a lot to be desired. I don't think my journal made it to MLK's birthday.

As we approached 2020, I knew that I had to do something different if I was going to be successful with this gratitude journal idea, and I needed to figure out why I hadn't been successful in the past.

In retrospect I probably had spent far too much time trying to decide what to write. Since hardly ever was there something of great significance to put on the list, and I didn't give much thought to the small things, my plan to keep a daily journal fizzled out pretty quickly. The reality of life, however, is that something outstanding doesn't occur every day. The tapestry of our lives is made up of inconsequential days. That's when a lightbulb turned on in my head and my view of a gratitude journal changed.

I've come to realize the obvious–that at the end of the day seldom has there been a wedding, or birth, or graduation, or a cure to a loved one's illness. Of course, I'm grateful for each of those fabulous days when they do occur, but they don't happen too often.

What is far more usual is that my life, our lives, are days sprinkled with smiles from strangers, helping hands from neighbors, hugs from family and friends, reminiscing with loved ones, and my dog going crazy with gladness to see me when I've only been gone for a few hours. I even discovered a day that I was grateful for honey mustard.

Most of my adult life I've made New Year's resolutions. If you do the same thing, you and I may share some of those resolutions. You know what I'm referring to–eat healthier meals, exercise on a regular basis, be nicer to a co-worker who isn't particularly nice, have more patience when you don't think you have any patience left, and the list goes on.

For some reason, I thought that if I added "write in a gratitude journal each day" to my New Year's resolutions that I would be more inclined to follow through with this goal. I totally believe that just like eating well and exercising are good resolutions for our physical health, that writing in a gratitude journal is good for our mental, emotional, and spiritual health. I've actually read that people who live with gratitude are happier and more optimistic people.

I'd like to share my gratitude journal with you from 2020. You'll see how even during the year of the pandemic, I was blessed to have much to be grateful for.

I hope that you were blessed, too.

JANUARY

January 1st

Taking walks each day is part of my daily routine. I'm grateful that I was able to walk 4.8 miles today. 10 years ago this would not have been possible.

January 2nd

One of Dave's best friends is the pastor of a church in Duncan, OK.

I'm grateful that each week Arnold sends me his church's bulletin. This week's bulletin had words that were particularly meaningful to me:

"The results we get from our best efforts may not always be what we imagined, or would have liked, but that doesn't make them wasted efforts."

I'm thankful to have read those words today.

January 3rd

My son, Michael, stopped by my house for a surprise visit. What mom wouldn't be grateful for that to happen?

January 4th

We are blessed to own two rental properties. One is the house that I grew up in. The other is the house that Dave and I bought when we were first married.

I thought that there was a homeowner's insurance payment due today for one of them. When I called the insurance company to make the payment, I was told that I have a -0- balance.

I was really grateful to hear that news!!!

January 5th

Gradually, I'm increasing how far I walk. I'm grateful that today I walked 5.0 miles.

January 6th

I'm grateful that my car insurance premium was reduced by $30.00. Everything helps.

January 7th

I attend Mass daily. I'm grateful that today at Mass there was the Anointing of the Sick.

Even though I feel great, and will always think that I'm healthy unless a doctor tells me otherwise, I take part in this sacrament whenever it's offered. I've done this ever since I came close to dying from complications of cancer treatment.

January 8th

My back has been bothering me for a while. Today when I saw the doctor he said that no shots or imaging would be necessary at this time. Instead, he gave me handouts of exercises to do.

I'm grateful for this simple solution.

January 9th

This evening my daughter, Kathleen, stopped by after work to say, "Hello." I have the best daughter ever!!!

January 10th

After my chemo and radiation treatments were over, I was put on a pill for five years that is a continued treatment for my breast cancer. There are enough side effects from this pill that I was relieved when my five years were behind me. That's when my oncologist told me that the newest findings show that women who stay on the pill for 10 years have a decreased likelihood that the cancer will return. Even though I was disappointed, I decided that I would rather put up with the side effects, and at the same time reduce the chances of the cancer returning.

One of the side effects is that it can cause osteoporosis. Before I started taking the pill, a baseline bone density test was done. I was happy to be told that my bones were classified as young adult. However, by the time I reached the five year mark, I was halfway through osteopenia heading towards osteoporosis.

One of the things that helps to improve bone density is weight bearing exercises. That is why taking walks and getting in as many steps each day as possible is particularly beneficial to me.

I am so grateful that my extra walking has paid off. Today I had a bone density test and I was told that the results were better than the last time I had the test. My bones are now denser and I'm closer to the normal range than I am to osteoporosis. Yay!

January 11th

When lunchtime was approaching, I thought that a tomato, avocado, and Swiss cheese sandwich on toasted bread with honey mustard dressing sounded really good.

Unfortunately, I didn't have any honey mustard, so I got into my car and headed to the nearby grocery store. I went directly to the aisle with the salad dressings and reached for the honey mustard. That's when I realized that there would still be plenty of dressing left in the bottle long after the expiration date had passed, and that I'd be throwing a lot of it away.

My next stop was the deli counter where I could buy a small container of honey mustard. The lady in line in front of me had just finished ordering what sounded like a delicious sandwich. I asked if she had ever had it before. She said that she had it many times in the past, and that it was really good. However, she said that it comes with honey mustard but that she likes it spicier so she orders it with spicy brown mustard.

I laughed and told her that the only reason that I was in line was to buy a take out container of honey mustard. She smiled at me, and then asked the gentleman who was making her sandwich to also put some honey mustard in the bag with her sandwich. When he gave it to her, she took the mustard out of the bag and handed it to me.

I was grateful for the honey mustard, but more so for what that lady had done. That small gesture by a stranger, her random act of kindness, touched my heart.

January 12th

Recently, one of the tenants living in my childhood home called to ask for permission to do something in the house. I told him that I would have to think about it. He and his wife and two young children are great tenants, and I didn't want to do anything that would cause them not to want to renew their lease.

I have to admit that my decision wasn't easy to make, and that I lost some sleep over it. Two weeks after his question, I made my decision. I called and left a detailed message on his voicemail denying his request. A few hours later when I saw his name on my caller ID I was concerned by what he might say.

He couldn't have been nicer when he said that they totally understood why I had made the decision that I made.

I'm grateful, and I'm relieved by his words.

January 13th

Today was the first time that I have walked any distance in several days because of the pain in my back. I'm starting to feel better and I'm grateful that the exercises that my doctor suggested are working.

January 14th

I had lunch today with my friend, Eileen. We've been friends since our daughters were little girls at our church's daycare. I'm grateful for all the happy times we've shared and celebrated together. I'm also grateful that we could understand each other's pain during our sad times. I'm grateful for our friendship.

January 15th

I've written a book titled *I'll Love Ye Forever: A Mother and Daughter's Journey Through Long Term Care*. While it's always nice to see on my Amazon reports that there have been sales, my main incentive is for the book to be read. If one person purchases the book and shares it with other people, I am grateful. Recently, I've been speaking at local churches about my personal experience with long term care.

Today I had a meeting with a couple of ladies from another church who are planning for me to speak at their church on the 1st of February.

I'm grateful and I'm blessed that they think my book is worth sharing with their congregation.

January 16th

I got a haircut today. I have natural curly hair. I totally believe that it takes a certain knack to be able to cut curly hair well. Cristina has been my hairdresser for many years and she has that knack. When I was going through chemo and my hair started to fall out, she went with me to help me pick out a wig, and to trim it so that it would look its best on my head.

I'm grateful that Cristina is the person who cuts my hair, but I'm even more grateful that we're friends.

January 17th

I recently had a new roof put on my home, as well as on one of the rentals. Today an inspector from a wind mitigation company went to the rental house to inspect the new roof. A copy of the inspector's report will be submitted to my homeowner's insurance company.

I'm grateful to Roofer Rick for telling me about this inspection. He has nothing to gain by me having this extra inspection which I paid for, but if he hadn't told me about it, I wouldn't have known about its benefits to me.

January 18th

My neighbor, Cathy, brought me a bag of recently picked oranges. I'm grateful for her kindness.

January 19th

A friend messaged me to say that a mutual friend of ours gave her my book about long term care as a birthday present. Her message felt like a gift to me!

January 20th

Even though I live in sunny Florida, the weather sometimes gets pretty nippy. This morning's cold weather brought to mind a memory of something that happened many times during my life with Dave.

No matter how early I had to leave for work, no matter how cold it was, he would always go out to my car before I did, and he'd start it up for a few minutes while he was getting the ice off my windows.

In the warm weather he would go out to my car before me, and he'd wipe the dew off the windows.

I always appreciated his kindness at the time, but today as I look back with gratitude I appreciate it even more.

January 21st

My son stopped by and we ate lunch together. My daughter texted me this evening to say, "I love you."

I am so grateful that they are my kids.

January 22nd

In the mail today I received the written report in reference to my bone density test. I was grateful that the report did indicate that my bone density had improved, but there were also words on the report referencing some of my vertebra that sounded ominous.

I googled the words, but there were no exact matches. I thought that the words that were closest to those on the report indicated tumors, which could either be malignant or benign.

It's been less than five years since Dave was diagnosed with stage 4 lung cancer that had metastasized to his spine. I was afraid that I might soon hear a similar diagnosis.

I immediately called and left a message for my oncologist. Several angst filled hours later, I received a call back. I was assured that the words on the report did not indicate that I had cancer.

I'm grateful beyond words for that good news.

January 23rd

Tonight was Bunco night. I'm grateful that I get to spend one evening a month with 11 awesome ladies whom I think of as friends. Four of us have been friends since high school. We use this dice game as the reason we get together, but we all know it's really about sharing good fellowship.

It was especially fun for me tonight because I had the most Buncos and won $30.00. Woohoo!

January 24th

I'm grateful for an email that I received from my homeowner's insurance company. It was about the report that they received from the wind mitigation company pertaining to my rental's roof. The email said that my annual premium is being reduced, and that they will be sending me a refund check for an overpayment that had been made.

January 25th

After my mom and dad had both passed away, the house that I grew up in just sat vacant for a long time because I couldn't bear the thought of selling it. Eventually, Dave and I decided to turn it into a rental.

The house has a septic tank, and it's important that once a month a box of septic tank treatment be poured into the toilet.

Today I dropped off a two month supply to the tenants. I am grateful that they do this bit of maintenance for me to keep the septic tank in good working condition.

January 26th

I'm grateful that my friend, Barb, is visiting me from out of town for the weekend. She was Kathleen's Girl Scout leader from kindergarten through her senior year in high school. Her daughter, Katie, is Kathleen's friend, but she now lives far away from us.

This evening Barb, Kathleen, and I went out to dinner. It was great fun catching up!

January 27th

My Aunt Delia was very much in my thoughts today. Even though she has passed away, I will always remember that today is her birthday.

She was not only my aunt, but also my godmother. When I grew up she was my friend. She was with me from the beginning of my life, and I was with her through the end of hers.

When Delia passed away she was nearly 102 years old, and she still had a sharp mind and a great sense of humor. She was an inspiration to me.

I will always be grateful for my Aunt Delia.

January 28th

Today's regularly scheduled six month appointment with the oncologist went well. During the prior appointment I had with her, she suggested that I start taking a prescription medication to help make my bones stronger. I told her that I wanted to hold off doing that and see if I could improve them by walking more. She said, "Okay."

I'm grateful that my stubbornness paid off. Due to the fact that my increased walking showed a marked improvement on my recent bone density test, the doctor no longer thinks that I need to take a prescription pill or a shot that would do the same thing that my walking has done.

Today I'm also grateful that Kathleen came over to my house and we ate lunch together, and that Michael called this evening to see how the appointment with the oncologist went.

I'm grateful and blessed.

January 29th

My friend, Kim, called to say that she flew back into town so that she can hear my presentation this weekend about my book. I'll be speaking at the church that she attends. Wow! She's quite a friend!!!

January 30th

I am grateful for a long and fulfilling career at the State Attorney's Office. I miss the people that I worked with, and I even miss the work. Once a month a group of retirees from the office now meet for lunch. Today we met at a local steakhouse restaurant.

I'm blessed to still have these friendships that started in the last century.

January 31st

I'm grateful for a call I received today from the host of a local TV show. She wants to do a television interview with me about my long term care book. I was thrilled to be speaking with her, and I told her that I would be honored to give an interview. She told me that she would get back with me to let me know what date it will be scheduled.

Here's "the rest of the story" behind today's gratitude entry.

Many years ago when I was a student at the University of Central Florida, this lady who now wants to interview me about my writing sat in front of me in a college writing class. I wouldn't say that we were friends, but by the time the semester was over I'd say that we were close acquaintances. During the course of today's conversation I asked if she remembered me. It probably goes without saying that she said, "No."

The professor who taught our writing class was a gentleman by the name of Roland Browne. Professor Browne would one day be my father-in-law, but at that point I hadn't even met his son.

FEBRUARY

February 1st

I'm grateful that I was invited to speak today about my book on long term care, and that my presentation was at the church where Dave and I were married.

The morning started with the pastor saying Mass in the chapel, followed by coffee and breakfast pastries in the large meeting room, which is where I spoke. I thought that my presentation went well, and there was a lot of audience participation. Some of the people who had comments said that they had a similar journey with a loved one. I'm hoping that one day this journey will be made easier.

Two things were a little different today from other talks that I've given. This was the first time that Kathleen and my daughter-in-law, Aaliya, were in the audience. Michael wasn't able to be there so Aaliya took my picture speaking from the lectern and sent it to him. He texted her back saying that he was a proud son.

The second thing that was different today was that when my presentation was over several people came up to me, one with tears in her eyes, and thanked me for speaking. Another lady said that she learned information that will help her with her parents.

As I write in my gratitude journal this evening, I'm grateful that I was given the opportunity to reach so many people and tell them about the journey I took with my mom through long term care. It's a day I'll remember for a long time.

February 2nd

A Facebook friend and a neighbor both asked me where they could get my long term care book. I told them that they can order it on Amazon.

I'm grateful that my book is doing well, but there's something missing. Dave lived the story with me, but he's no longer here. Can I be grateful and sad at the same time? I think that answer is "yes" because today I feel both.

February 3rd

Kathleen's cat, Tiger, is nearly 20 years old. I am grateful and relieved that at today's checkup with the vet, the doctor said that he's healthy. I'm so happy to hear that great news!

February 4th

I sincerely appreciate the two email messages that I received from Lori and Kim, the ladies who planned my presentation on Saturday. I'm grateful for their kind words:

Lori wrote, "BIG THANK YOU to you Sally for sharing your beautiful, honest, heartfelt story."

Kim wrote, "It was a pleasure on every level! I am so happy to have found your book...and then you! I know your story touched so many and stirred something important in our parishioners on Saturday. I believe that many are hungry to share, discuss, and lend support on this matter–I'm so happy that we could bring you here."

February 5th

I was contacted by the leader of a Caregivers' Support Group asking if I would speak with the members. I quickly responded that I would love to do it. She said that she'll get back with me when she decides on a date. I am grateful to have been asked.

February 6th

The main library in my city has an annual Author's Festival. I applied to take part in the event, and today I was contacted and told that I was approved.

They weren't sure if this year's festival will happen in April or July, but either way I'm grateful that I will get to take part in it.

February 7th

Once a month I attend a get-together called "Cooking for One." Usually there are about 10 people who show up. It is meant for people who have lost their spouse, and who are used to cooking for more than one person.

Each month there is a different tasty meal that is cooked. When it comes out of the oven we serve ourselves, and then head to a long table in the dining area where there is always a great conversation.

I'm grateful for the camaraderie, and to be around people who understand what it feels like to have lost their spouse, to be cooking for one, and to be eating each day by yourself without your spouse sitting next to you at the table.

February 8th

Today I received a beautiful card from my cousin, Ireland. Later in the day my neighbor, Cathy, brought me roses from her garden.

I'm grateful to know that my family and friends think about me.

February 9th

My friend, Debra, told me that one of her friends saw my recent book presentation, and she said that she "absolutely loved it."

I'm grateful that Debra shared those encouraging words with me.

February 10th

I had my annual chest x-ray today. That's because my medical oncologist has told me that one of the places that breast cancer metastasizes to is the lungs.

I was happy, relieved, grateful, and blessed when I was told that my x-ray looked normal.

February 11th

Today I went to the movies and saw *Little Women* with Maryellen, Julie, and Pamm.

I'm grateful that they've been my friends since the 9th grade.

February 12th

Holy Moly!!! It's official! I received an email from the TV host who wants to do an interview with me about my long term care book. She said that the interview is scheduled for April 8th.

I'm grateful, blessed, and super excited!

February 13th

I'm grateful for the beautiful rainbow that I saw over the lake that I live on.

February 14th

I received Happy Valentine's Day texts from Kathleen and from Aaliya. It warms my heart, and I'm grateful that they remembered that this is a tough day for me.

February 15th

I saw a picture today that I had posted on Facebook from the last Valentine's Day that Dave was alive. We didn't know at the time that it would be our last one together. It was a picture of red roses in a beautiful crystal vase, next to a red heart-shaped box full of chocolates. They were his gifts to me.

When I posted the picture I wrote, "Thank you, Dave, for the beautiful flowers and candy. You've been my Valentine for the last 38 years. Let's go for 38 more. ILY most!"

As I write in my journal for today, I'm grateful for those 38 years with my best friend.

February 16th

After Mass today I ran into a friend who told me that she recently saw a TV interview with me about my book. It was an interview that was done last year with CCTN (Catholic Community Television Network). She made me laugh out loud when she said that I was a star.

I know that she was joking, but I was grateful for the laugh.

February 17th

This evening when I picked up Kathleen from the airport, I had the good fortune of running into three police officers that I used to work with when I worked at the State Attorney's Office. It was awesome to get to visit with these men who risk their lives daily keeping our city safe.

I'm grateful that my daughter is safely home, and that I happened to be at the same place, at the same time, to visit with my friends in blue.

February 18th

Today I'm grateful that I attended a seminar at my church called "Brain Fit and Healthy." I thought that it was interesting, informative, and helpful. When the speaker asked what we do for spirituality, I raised my hand and said that I wasn't sure if this was the type of answer that she was looking for, and then I told her about my gratitude journal.

She said that was a great answer. When the seminar was over a couple of people thanked me for giving them that idea. They said that they'd never thought of doing one, and that they'd give it a try.

If I remotely made a positive difference in someone's life, I am even more grateful that I attended the seminar.

February 19th

Tonight was the first night of a six-week bereavement class at my church. We'll meet once a week for the next six weeks. It's not just for people who have lost their spouse; it's for people who have lost anyone that they loved.

This isn't the first time that I've attended this series of classes. It's actually the third time. Even though the six weeks covers the same material each time, each time it's been different for me because there is a different group of people attending, with different situations and perspectives.

The class has helped me tremendously in spite of the fact that I don't easily open up to strangers about my personal thoughts and feelings.

I am so very grateful for the class, and that those who run it have allowed me to attend it three times.

February 20th

Bunco night! I'm grateful that my friend, Julie, drove to my house and that we then drove together to the hostess's house. Our ride together gave us time to update each other on what's been happening since the last Bunco meeting.

There is no skill to playing Bunco. I just happened to be lucky tonight and had "the traveler" at the end of the evening, and for that I won $5.00.

I'm grateful for all my Bunco friends, and for an extra $5.00.

February 21st

Today I had the opportunity to attend a town hall meeting with my congresswoman. She seemed sincere in listening to the concerns of the attendees who brought up issues.

I'm grateful that I live in a country that affords me the opportunity to meet face to face with the person who represents me, and who is working to make my community a better place to live. I know that there are many parts of the world where people aren't blessed in this manner.

February 22nd

Kevin is the person who mows my lawn. Dave hired him years ago to mow, edge, and blow off the driveway. He did everything else himself. Unlike Dave, I'm not skilled enough or knowledgeable enough to do the many other things that sometimes need to be done involving lawn maintenance, even the simple things.

Kevin never says, "No" to my requests and does them without blinking an eye. Today I needed one of those simple things done so that my grass wouldn't die. I needed a sprinkler head changed, which Kevin did before he went to his next job.

I'm sincerely grateful for all his help.

February 23rd

A couple years before Dave passed away we bought a condo near the beach. It needed a lot of work to be done, so on most Saturday mornings we drove two hours to get to it, did some work, ate a lovely dinner at the beach, and returned back home late on Saturday night. We finished a good deal of what needed to be done before Dave passed away. Our plan was that the condo would be a weekend getaway or a destination for vacations. I will always regret that Dave didn't get to use it like we had planned.

Today as I write in my journal I am filled with gratitude that I still have the condo. I'm equally grateful for my cousin, Sally. If it wasn't for her, I'd often be up the creek since I don't live in or near the condo. She lives in her condo that is located in the same building as mine.

Sally helps me tremendously by letting in the person who does the annual maintenance on the air conditioning system; she pours vinegar in the AC unit each month to keep it in good working condition; she lets in the worker who cleans out the dryer vent; she was there when the repairman came to fix my stove; she helped Kathleen when she arrived at the condo late one weekend night with car problems; and the list goes on.

My cousin, Sally, is a blessing to her cousin, Sally.

February 24th

The wind mitigation inspection for the roof on the house that I live in has given me reason to be grateful. I was notified today that my mortgage company has reduced my monthly mortgage payment. Additionally, they are sending me a check for an overpayment.

I continue to be grateful to Roofer Rick for suggesting the wind mitigation inspection. That suggestion has saved me money on my home, and also on my rental.

February 25th

I had breakfast at a restaurant today with my friend, Gail. We've been good friends since our daughters became BFFs when they were toddlers at our church's daycare. That was a long time ago.

I am grateful for our long, adventurous, and supportive friendship throughout the years.

February 26th

Today is Michael's birthday. He's the reason that Dave and I went from being a couple to being a family.

I am blessed and will always be grateful to the end of my days that he's my son.

February 27th

I'm grateful for a lady by the name of Liya. I've never met her, but she went above and beyond to help me today. She works in customer service for my internet provider. I was having problems with my internet and she patiently walked me through what I needed to do to reconnect my service.

I guess I'm a dinosaur because I still have a landline telephone, in addition to my cell phone. Not only did Liya resolve the problem with my internet, she did something so that now when I get a call on my landline, I have caller ID visible on my TV. Additionally, I'll no longer be getting robocalls on my landline. I'm grateful for that news, too!

February 28th

Today is a day that I'm overflowing with gratitude.

Weeks ago I had some routine blood work done, and the results gave me reason to be a little concerned. My potassium level was at 5.8. When I checked with "Dr. Google" it said that a potassium level higher than 5.5 is critically high, and over 6.0 can be life-threatening.

When I called my doctor he told me that false results from a potassium test are possible. He said that he wanted to do the test again in a few weeks, which took place earlier this week. He called me today with the new results which are 4.0. That's totally within the normal range. He wants me to repeat the test one more time when I have my physical in a few months.

My doctor's call to me today was the reason for a huge sigh of relief, and prayers of thanksgiving.

February 29th

I received a text today from the tenants renting my childhood home. The message was from the wife asking permission to get a pet. Dave and I had been asked that same question by an earlier tenant and we said, "Yes." When that family moved out a few years later, we were disappointed when we saw that their dog had caused a lot of damage. We decided at that time that we would no longer allow pets.

I felt bad today when I told the wife that they couldn't get a pet, but I was grateful that it was easier than last month when I told her husband that they couldn't do something that he had asked permission to do. That's because I knew what Dave would say if he was alive since he and I made this pet decision together, not all that long ago.

MARCH

March 1st

I'm grateful for a memory that came to mind today. It has to do with Amazon and my first book's ranking. Typically, the rankings change hourly. I don't pay much attention to them, however, because it's not something that I can control.

Timing is everything, and there was a moment in time that I happened to look at the ranking just at the right moment. I was blown away to see that my book was ranked at #70. That in itself is awesome! The icing on the cake was that my book was ranked right next to a book by Billy Graham. His book was ranked at #71. I quickly took a screenshot of something that I never could have imagined.

March 2nd

I haven't mentioned being grateful for my dog, Molly. That's because I could write her name on my gratitude list 365 days a year.

Eight years ago when we had to put our beloved Seamus to sleep, somehow on the quiet drive home from the vet Dave convinced me to stop by the pet store that was having pet adoptions. He promised me that we were only going to look, and that it would make us feel better to see the puppies. What was I thinking?

Hours after Dave, Kathleen, and I walked into the store, we left having signed adoption papers for a shy little black Lab mix puppy. I will be forever grateful that I agreed to getting this fur baby. I don't know what I would do without her.

March 3rd

I "think" that I'm grateful for something out of the ordinary that happened today, but then again, it brought tears to my eyes.

I wasn't able to find my cell phone. When I couldn't find my phone when Dave was alive, or the kids still lived at home, I'd ask one of them to call my number from their cell phone. Since I now live by myself, I just call my number from the landline.

When I did that today I heard my cell phone ringing and quickly located it. Typically, my home phone number would show on my cell's caller ID. Today it stunningly said "David Browne."

My heart skipped a beat, and for a nanosecond I thought that Dave was calling me. Yes, I'm grateful for that nanosecond.

March 4th

I'm grateful for the second meeting of the bereavement class. I've been looking forward to it since our first session. Sharing my grief with others who are going through many of the same emotions as I am makes this grieving process a little easier.

I invited a friend to come with me this evening. She, too, has lost her husband after a long marriage. I was happy to hear that Mary Beth thought that the class was helpful.

March 5th

Cooking for One class—I'm grateful for the company of this group of people who have lost their spouses. Unlike the bereavement class, Cooking for One will not end after a certain number of classes.

I hope that the ladies who run this class realize just how much of a positive impact they're having on those of us who attend. The food is good, but I don't think this really is about the food.

March 6th

I'm grateful that I finally finished putting together all that is needed to bring to the accountant for my taxes.

It's weird to say "my" taxes when for the majority of my life it was "our" taxes. Who would have thought that a pronoun could make me a little sad?

The flip side is that I'm blessed that I was able to use two pronouns for nearly 40 years when I referred to Dave and me. I'm grateful to have been a "we" and an "us" with him.

March 7th

There's a virus that's been in the news a lot lately. It's called COVID- 19, and it's deadly.

Today when I attended Mass, the pastor told us about some of the changes that will be implemented to keep the parishioners safe when coming to Mass. There will no longer be holy water fonts in the church; we are no longer allowed to touch each other during the sign of peace–no hugging or shaking hands; and only the host will be given during Communion.

I'm grateful for these precautions.

March 8th

Today when Kathleen stopped by for a visit, she surprised me with a basil plant. She knows how much I love to use fresh basil in my cooking. She also brought me a flavored coffee–yummy. And she brushed Molly's teeth and gave her a bath.

I'm grateful to have been blessed with such a kind and loving daughter.

March 9th

I'm grateful to have met my friend, Lucy, for dinner. We were having such a great time, and we were so into our conversation that it wasn't until the end of the evening that we noticed that we were the only ones left in the restaurant.

I think that's a sign of a good friend.

March 10th

I'm grateful for my friend, Maryellen. We've been friends since we were in high school. When we were in college we had a fun job working together at a movie theater.

Today we had lunch together across the street from that same movie theater where we worked decades ago.

As enjoyable as our lunch was today, however, I think that this may be my last restaurant meal for a while. COVID- 19 is starting to make me nervous.

March 11th

Today is the day of the week that I'm grateful for the bereavement class at my church. I continue to receive comfort from each meeting, and I am grateful that my church has developed this ministry for those of us who need it.

I was glad that my friend, Mary Beth, attended the class with me again tonight, and that she, too, finds it a blessing.

March 12th

Annissa is a former co-worker that I worked with over 10 years ago. Today she posted words on Facebook that touched my heart. She wrote "You made work a joy. You deserve all the joy in the world."

How could I not be grateful for someone to think that way about me, and to remember those feelings so many years later?

March 13th

I'm grateful that my friend, Kim, called me today and that we had a long chat.

We met years ago when her dad and my aunt had been in the same long term care facility. We each visited our loved ones daily for years, and through those tough times Kim and I became lifelong friends. We even kept an eye on each other's loved one, if the other was going to be out of town. Her dad and my aunt have each passed away, but she and I continue to be friends.

It's been a while since we've seen each other, but for now phone calls will probably have to suffice. I'm happy that I got to hear Kim's voice today and to know that she's doing well.

March 14th

I'm happy for a call that I received today from Michael. He called to see how I was doing and to make sure that I was safely getting out of my house each day.

I know how busy he is in nursing school, working full time at the hospital, being a husband, and being a first time homeowner. I'm grateful that he finds time for me, too.

March 15th

Today I'm grateful for memories of basketball.

Kathleen was on the Rollins College Women's Basketball Team. Dave and I seldom missed a game during her four years on the team as we made memories that will last a lifetime. Her team had four trips to the second round of the NCAA tournament, two Sunshine State Conference Championships, one SSC regular season title, and the program's first NCAA Final Four.

Basketball came to mind today because this is the time of the year that college basketball teams are playing in March Madness. This year, however, due to the pandemic, March Madness has been cancelled. I sincerely feel bad for the teams, coaches, and families who will not be able to take part in this wonderful event. I know how important this is for all those involved.

When Kathleen's team made it to the Sweet 16, Dave and I drove from Florida to Texas to get to watch them play in the tournament. I will always remember the game that they won that brought them to the Final Four. When the buzzer went off at the end of the game, I couldn't stop crying.

I was crying tears of happiness not just because we won, but because I was so thankful to be at the tournament at all. I kept thinking how blessed I was that I had beaten cancer and the complications that nearly took my life.

This evening as I write in my journal and I think about this memory, I'm so grateful that Dave was by my side for this March Madness, and that we got to experience this joy together.

Each day is a gift.

March 16th

I stopped by Kathleen's office this morning for no reason, and I surprised her with a chocolate croissant. She later texted me to say, "Thank you so much!!! You are seriously The Best, and you made my Monday start off great!"

I'm grateful that such a small gesture on my part could make my daughter happy.

March 17th

Today is St. Patrick's Day, and when I woke up this morning I thought about how grateful I am for my Irish roots. I recently found out that because my mom was born in Ireland, I automatically have dual citizenship. I consider myself blessed that I still have many close relatives who live on the Emerald Isle, and that throughout the years I've taken many trips there with my mom, Dave, Michael, and Kathleen. Whenever we visit I always feel like I'm going home.

Early this morning I was happy to see that my cousin, Gearoidin in Ireland, emailed me her recipe for potato/leek soup. It sounds delicious, and I will definitely be making it. I also noticed that corned beef is on sale today for half price. I couldn't pass up that sort of a bargain, so I made a trip to the grocery store and picked one up, along with cabbage and potatoes.

Due to the pandemic, I ate supper by myself but I'm still grateful that my traditional Irish supper was so very delicious.

March 18th

Due to the pandemic, changes are happening that will impact me. I'm not happy about any of them, but they are all necessary.

I have attended daily Mass for many years. Today was the last Mass that will be held in my church until COVID- 19 is under control. Starting tomorrow Mass will be livestreamed. It won't be the same, but I'm grateful for what it is.

The weekly bereavement classes have also been cancelled; Bunco has been cancelled; the Cooking for One classes have been cancelled, too.

I'm grateful that my neighbor, Cathy, left a pretty white rose on my doorstep that she had picked from her garden. Her thoughtfulness balanced the not so great news from earlier in the day.

March 19th

Tonight would have been Bunco. When I told Kathleen that it had been cancelled, she stopped by my house on her way home from work and brought me an iced coffee. She knows how much I like them.

Next, we socially distanced ourselves by each driving our own car to a nearby park for a scenic walk, and some good mom/daughter talk. Molly came along, too.

I'm grateful. I'm blessed.

March 20th

I'm grateful that I completed the census, and that I can take it off my to-do list.

March 21st

I always enjoy my morning walk but today perhaps more so than usual. The weather was great which was probably the reason that many people were working in their yards. I had a nice chitchat with three of them. The human contact during this time of isolation sincerely brightened my spirits.

Several blocks from my house I even shared the sidewalk for a bit of the way with a big turtle that probably came from the lake that I live on.

Today I'm grateful for friendly people, and for a friendly turtle, too.

March 22nd

I totally messed up the remote control to my TV. I don't have a clue what button or buttons I pressed, but I couldn't figure out how to fix it. It's not that I couldn't get up and do all the things we used to have to do before remote controls were invented, it's that the TV wouldn't let me do it.

I called Kathleen and I'm grateful that she calmly and patiently walked me through how to fix the problem that I'd created. The two words that I'm most grateful for are calmly and patiently.

March 23rd

I did a lot of yardwork today at one of the rentals. It was hard work, and I'm glad that it's done. I'm grateful to Cathy who helped me with the work. That kindness goes above and beyond being a good neighbor.

I'm also grateful that the tenant texted me to say, "Thank you. It looks beautiful."

March 24th

I am so grateful that over the last few days, I've heard from three of my cousins–Paula, Barbara, and Rose.

We had lost contact with each other for decades, and we've only reconnected in recent years. We were able to rekindle our relationships where we left off. It's wonderful!!!

March 25th

I have to admit that some days during the pandemic have been a little tougher than others, but somehow something good happens every day that causes me to be grateful. Today was one of those days.

I really wanted and needed to get my hair trimmed before my TV interview that was scheduled to happen on April 8th. The problem is that all the hair salons are closed until further notice.

Problem solved–The host of the show called me today to say that due to COVID- 19 they were cancelling my interview. I'm disappointed that the interview has been cancelled, but I'm grateful that when it gets rescheduled, my book will be more relevant than it presently is, and that hopefully I'll look more presentable than I'll look on April 8th.

March 26th

I am so grateful that during the Stay At Home Order that I have a comfortable home to live in. Even though it's sometimes lonely being the only person in my home, I know that I'm blessed. Many people have no home at all.

March 27th

Michael texted me to say that he misses me. I'm hugely grateful for his heartfelt message.

March 28th

I can't say strongly enough how grateful I am that when my mom and aunt were living in their respective long term care facilities that it wasn't during a pandemic. For years I visited them daily, and I honestly don't know how they would have handled this lockdown without me being with them every day. It was tough enough for them during the best of conditions.

I no longer have a loved one living in a facility, but I pray for those people living in one, as well as their families. I also pray for the people who are taking care of them.

March 29th

I'm grateful that even though it's March, my Christmas cactus is still blooming.

March 30th

Over the weekend I did a lot of yardwork at my house. I filled several large bags with leaves, and weeds, and trimmed bush branches. I put the bags at the end of my driveway for the garbagemen to take away. Today I am grateful for those hardworking men who were kind enough to dispose of those bags, along with a can filled with regular garbage.

It wasn't until I saw them putting my trash into their truck that my pandemic brain realized that today wasn't the scheduled day for yard waste. I ran to the end of my driveway to apologize for putting the yard waste there on the wrong day and to thank the men for their kindness. The driver of the truck told me that it was okay, and that he would always take care of me.

March 31st

I received a call today from the tenants who live in the house that Dave and I bought when we were newlyweds. The wife said that they were having plumbing problems. I immediately called and left a detailed message with the plumber. Within minutes he returned my call and said that he would go to their home today.

Later in the day I received another call from the tenant saying that the plumber had been to their home, got up on the roof, diagnosed the problem, and fixed it. All is now well. I am so grateful for our reliable plumber, Jim.

By the way, Jim is 85 years young.

APRIL

April 1st

Today is April Fools' Day. This morning I got a text from Michael saying, "It's snowing at St. Mary Magdalen." That's the name of our church and the name of the school that he went to when he was a little boy. Since we live in Florida, there really is "a snowball's chance in hell" that it would snow at St. Mary Magdalen.

However, many moons ago on April Fools' Day that's exactly what I said to him when I woke him up for school. It wasn't until I was driving him there that I blurted out "April Fool."

It makes me smile that all these years later Michael still remembers this joke between him and me.

April 2nd

Kathleen called to ask if I needed anything from the store. I thanked her for asking and then told her that I had everything that I needed. A few hours later she stopped by my house with treats for Molly that were BOGO.

I'm grateful for Kathleen, Molly, and BOGOs.

April 3rd

Once again my internet wasn't working. I'm grateful to Malcolm, the masked technician who spent more than four hours at my house restoring my internet.

April 4th

I'm grateful that Michelle is my sister-in-law, and that she's always so thoughtful. She called me today just to say, "Hello" and to see how I'm doing.

April 5th

Today I'm grateful that I received an email from my auto insurance company saying that due to the pandemic they were lowering my premium by 15%.

April 6th

Theresa is one of my tenants. She's dealing with cancer. Somewhere over the years she went from being not only a tenant, but also a friend. She texted me today to say that she had surgery, and that it went well.

I am both delighted and grateful to know this encouraging news.

April 7th

I'm thankful that I wasn't run over today by a wackadoo.

I needed to speak with my lawn service before they started mowing my lawn today. I noticed that their truck was parked a few houses up the street. At the same time I noticed them, I also saw a strange car parked in my driveway. As I walked down my driveway the man inside the car just kept staring straight ahead, with both hands on his steering wheel. I walked quickly past him and went to speak with the lawn man. My back was to my house and to the stranger's car. Suddenly, the lawn man hollered to me, "Get out of the way."

The wackadoo had put his car in reverse and stepped on the accelerator. He barely missed hitting the back of the lawn service truck by inches. Through his closed windows and with my hands on my hips, I told him to put his window down. I curtly asked him what he was trying to do.

He told me that he was sorry, and that he didn't mean to scare me. Then he asked how to get out of there.

The lawn man said, "Scare us? You nearly hit us with your car." Then he told him to go around the cul-de-sac and that would lead him off the street.

Mr. Wackadoo took him literally, and he drove his car around the cul-de-sac three times before heading up the street.

I'm grateful that things turned out the way they did. It could have had a totally different ending.

April 8th

Long before I had breast cancer, I had a melanoma. I've lost relatives to this serious type of skin cancer so I know how deadly it can be. For the rest of my life, I have to see my dermatologist every three to four months for a complete body check. Today was my appointment.

I am so very grateful that my doctor, who only sees patients with a history of skin cancer, said that he didn't see anything to be concerned about. Phew!

April 9th

Today I went to the hardware store to buy air conditioning filters. I looked and I looked for the unusual size that I needed, but I couldn't find the size that I was looking for.

Bucky, one of the store's employees, walked down the aisle where I had already spent far too much time, and he asked if he could help me find something. As soon as I told him what I needed, he quickly picked one up and handed it to me.

I'm grateful for Bucky's help.

April 10th

Today is Good Friday, and it was good. I'm grateful that I was able to watch the Passion of Christ Mass as it was livestreamed. During the Mass I prayed for my family, and friends, and for Molly.

I dropped her off at her vet's clinic this morning at 7:30 because she was going to have dental surgery to remove several teeth. She's always had an underbite that gave her a unique look. It was part of her personality, and we all loved her cute face. The veterinarian was concerned, however, that the teeth that were her underbite were all loose, and she said they should be removed. She was also concerned about the health of her jawbone.

I was apprehensive how the surgery would turn out. Due to COVID- 19, I couldn't go inside the clinic with her which didn't make my timid dog happy.

Late in the afternoon I received a call from the vet. She said that the surgery went well, and that Molly's jawbone appeared healthy. She said that I could come and pick her up.

I have so much to be grateful for every day. Today I'm especially grateful for Molly, and for her good health. I'd be lost without her.

April 11th

Michael explained in detail how to use Zoom. I'm grateful that he was patient with his technologically challenged mother, and that I learned something new.

April 12th

Today is Easter. I'm sure missing Dave and all the traditions that go along with a non-pandemic Easter. However, a lot happened today that I'm grateful for.

Michael and Aaliya came by for a visit and brought me candy; Kathleen later stopped by and gave me a pretty mosaic bunny and a chocolate bunny; and Cathy brought me Easter lilies from her garden. I'm grateful for all their thoughtfulness, but I'm most grateful that they gave me their time.

During the pandemic we're all coming up with ways to stay connected with our loved ones. For us today, there was an Easter Zoom family dinner meeting.

I'm grateful for my loving family, and that there is an Easter.

April 13th

My cousin, Shaun, died today from COVID- 19. It's tough to think of a reason to be grateful after hearing this sad news, but I'll try.

When I was a child we lived in New Jersey. Shaun and his family lived in New York, and on the weekends we'd sometimes visit them. I remember him as being a sweet boy. He grew up to be a kind and sweet man.

A few years ago, Kathleen and I flew to New York to attend Shaun's nephew's wedding. I'm grateful that I got to spend some time with Shaun that weekend.

I'm grateful that he was my cousin.

April 14th

I had my yearly physical today with the doctor who found my cancerous breast tumor 11 years ago. Today I was grateful to hear him say that I'm in really good shape, and that I have a strong immune system. There's not much better news to hear than that of good health.

April 15th

Today my neighbor, George, did something that reminded me what great neighbors I have. For no reason, other than the goodness of his heart, he cut dead fronds from my palm tree.

I'm grateful and lucky that George and Flo are my neighbors.

April 16th

Today when I was looking at old photographs of my family, I was grateful that I noticed the obvious for the first time in one of those pictures.

I saw eight relationships–husband, wife, father, mother, son, daughter, brother, and sister.

I saw four individuals–Dave, Sally, Michael, and Kathleen.

I saw one family–us.

April 17th

I'm grateful for whatever motivated me to make Irish soda bread today. It was the first time that I tried making it, and as I kneaded it I could almost hear my mom, with her thick Irish brogue, saying, "There's a first time for everything."

I gave some of it to Kathleen this evening. She took it home with her, and later texted me to say that she put Irish butter on it, and that it was delicious!

I sure wish I could share it with Dave, and my mom and dad, and my Aunt Delia. I think that they would have liked it, too.

April 18th

I've found that sometimes during the toughest of times there are still reasons to be grateful. Today I thought about a person whose kindness helped me during one of my challenging times.

Before I met Dave I had only spent one afternoon on a sailboat. During our four decades together, however, sailing became a big part of our lives, and our kids' lives, too. Dave's dad had taught Dave and his brother, John, how to sail when they were youngsters. When they grew up John bought a large sailboat. Somehow, Dave convinced me that we should do the same.

We enjoyed sailing our boat for many years prior to Dave having her trucked from the marina to the end of our driveway. That is where he planned to do a major overhaul and renovation. He was respectful of the neighbors and never worked on our boat early in the mornings or late in the evenings. While the sound of drilling and sawing was minimal, he didn't want to disturb anyone.

The neighbor on the other side of our tall fence, however, must have been troubled by Dave's work and turned us into Code Enforcement shortly after Dave had passed away. I don't know why he chose that time to do what he did.

The Violation that I received said that our boat could no longer remain on our property unless she was on a trailer, or moved into the garage. The boat was too big to do either of those things. The Violation said that I had 16 days to resolve the problem, or I would be fined more than $200.00 a day.

When I spoke with the Code Enforcement Officer, she told me that she had seen my husband working on the boat for a few years. She said she would never have done anything, but because the neighbor had filed a formal complaint she had to give me the Violation.

I had just lost Dave and then soon after his death I was having to figure out what to do with our boat. Sadly, I knew that I would have to get rid of her. I tried donating her to several colleges on the coast around the country. A few were interested but each wanted me to pay for the cost of transporting her, which I didn't want to do.

My only other choice was to sell her. I thought that would probably be a challenge because Dave had only gotten halfway through the overhaul project.

I was incredibly sad at what I had to do, but at the same time I was thankful that the officer had extended the time limit not just once, but twice. She had given me more than five months in total. This gave me more time to find someone who wanted to buy our boat, and who was willing and able to do all the necessary work to get her back in the water.

I'll be forever grateful to this officer who initially was a stranger to me, but who helped me more than words can say.

April 19th

I'm grateful and blessed that a Facebook friend wrote that I was a blessing to many people. I don't know if that's true, but what a wonderful thing to read.

April 20th

I'm heartbroken for my cousin, Rose, who lost her husband to COVID-19. I'm grateful that I was able to watch Steven's memorial service this evening on Zoom, and "be with my family" even though we're thousands of miles apart.

April 21st

I'm grateful for a cool and breezy morning. It was a wonderful change from the heat and humidity that we've been having.

April 22nd

I am grateful that today I received a message from LinkedIn saying that one of my posts was trending–#dementia. I'm not exactly sure what trending means, but I take it to be a good thing.

April 23rd

I'm grateful that my friend, Charlie, asked if Kathleen or I needed a face mask to protect us from the virus. I told him that we both did.

When he said that his wife, Tina, was making masks I told him that I would like to buy a couple from her. He told me that she doesn't charge for her masks, but she gives them away to those who need them.

I am so very grateful for the pretty masks that Tina made for us, and for her kindness.

April 24th

I'm grateful that prayers have been answered for my former colleague, Kevin, who had been on total life support and in a medically induced coma battling COVID-19.

A man who didn't even know Kevin saw a plea on Facebook asking for someone who had recovered from the virus to please donate their plasma, which has lifesaving antibodies. The stranger was tested and was a match. The following day he traveled hundreds of miles so that the donation could be made.

It was only a matter of days after Kevin received this gift of life that he was taken out of the medically induced coma and off life support. He's now home with his family.

I'm grateful for my friend's recovery and for the stranger who saved his life.

April 25th

One of my tenants texted me to say, "Thank you for being you." I'm grateful that she thinks that way about me.

April 26th

I'm grateful that the IRS site indicates that I will be receiving a stimulus check.

April 27th

Today is John's birthday. He's Dave's only brother.

I will always be grateful that he's my brother-in-law. Even though he lives on the opposite side of the country from me, he's my "go to" person whenever I have concerns about things that Dave would have handled.

John has answered my questions about maintenance issues with the houses and with my car; he's given me advice when I was over-the-top stressed about our sailboat; and he was the person who handled all the technical parts of getting my first book published.

I'm grateful that we're family, and I'm grateful to know that we're only a phone call, a text, or an email away.

April 28th

I'm grateful that I motivated myself to go through stacks of papers that kept getting taller, and to dispose of what I didn't need. Then I filed away the rest, just in case I'll need any of them in the future. It's a feeling of accomplishment that I'm grateful to have today.

April 29th

My cousin, Marty, called me today. When my mom and our aunt were in their 80s and 90s, and even over a 100 years old, Marty used to call them all the time, too. Those phone calls put smiles on their faces and let them know that he was thinking about them.

I'm grateful for Marty, and that he's my family and my friend.

April 30th

My friend, Gail, texted me to invite me to go out for tea with her when the pandemic is over.

I'm grateful for her text, her friendship, and for something fun to look forward to.

MAY

May 1st

Today I'm grateful once again for our plumber, Jim, and for something that happened while he was at my house today.

When he was about to start fixing the plumbing problem, he asked if I'd go outside and turn off the water to the house. I had been in that area outside of the house earlier in the day, and everything was fine. When I went outside to turn off the water, however, I saw that water was gushing from one of the pipes. I quickly turned off the water, and then I went inside to tell Jim.

He fixed the problem that I had called him for, and then he fixed the outside pipe which had nothing to do with the original problem.

I'm grateful not only that Jim is our plumber, but that the pipe broke while he was at my house. What are the chances of that happening?

May 2nd

I don't have city water at my house. We had the option of hooking up to city water a few years ago while Dave was still alive, but we made the decision to continue using our well water which comes from the aquifer, and which tastes delicious.

Shortly after Jim left my house yesterday, I discovered a second leak near the pipe he had fixed. This one was from a gasket going into one of the well's pressure tanks.

I called Jim and explained the problem. He said that problem had nothing to do with my house's plumbing, but was totally well related, and that I needed to contact the person who works on issues with our well.

So ... I called Floyd, the well expert, and today he came to my house and fixed the leak. I'm grateful that Floyd not only fixed the leak, but also that he refused to charge me.

My heart continues to be touched by the kindness that people show me.

May 3rd

Today is Kathleen's birthday. I am so grateful and blessed that she's my daughter. Even though it's her birthday, she brought me a gift of delicious homemade bread that she'd made. Usually we all go out as a family for our birthdays to celebrate the birthday person, but due to the pandemic it wasn't an option this year for Kathleen. This evening we had a Zoom birthday dinner celebration in her honor. When the pandemic is behind us, we'll celebrate her birthday in a more festive way.

May 4th

On my back porch I have three beautiful orchid plants that start blooming every year between Easter and Mother's Day. They make me happy when I look at them, and I'm blessed that they continue to bloom for months. They were gifts from Dave that he gave to me in different years. Since he's been gone, each year when they begin to bloom I get the same wonderful feeling that I got each of the three times that he gave them to me.

I am so very grateful for these beautiful flowers that I get each year from Dave.

May 5th

I'm grateful that shortly after Dave passed away I found Fern, a handyman who does great work at an affordable price, and whom I can trust. He's done everything from small jobs that I don't know how to do, to big jobs that I can't do like repairing major damage caused by a hurricane.

Today when he was doing some work at my house I realized that he's not just my handyman; he's become a friend.

May 6th

Dave was talented in so many ways. One of his talents was woodworking. He built our first bedroom furniture—two dressers, two bedside tables, and a headboard. He also built bunk beds for our kids when they were small, and a desk, and parts for our sailboat.

Today as I walked quickly through my living room something caught my eye that was hanging on the wall that I hadn't paid much attention to in a long time. It's a printer's box that Dave built for me during our dating days. It's filled with memorabilia that's meaningful to me. I'll mention just a few of them–a little painted porcelain tea cup from my tea set from when I was a little girl, a heavy copper paperweight of a bear that I remember playing with as a child, a souvenir from The Old Curiosity Shop in England that I bought when I was in college, a small candle that a teenage boyfriend bought me on a date at Walt Disney World, two printer blocks with the letters S and B that a friend gave me shortly before I got married when they were about to become my new initials, two rabbits sitting on a park bench kissing that reminded me of Dave and me, a button that says, "It's A Boy–Mike," a die that Dave brought back from a business trip to Las Vegas, and at the top of the printer's box is my name plate that hung outside my work office for many years.

I'm grateful that today in my living room I slowed down long enough to "stop and smell the roses." I'm also grateful that once upon a time Dave built me this treasure that literally holds some of my fond memories.

May 7th

I've been worried about a letter I recently received that said that next month my surgical oncologist will be leaving the Medical Center that he's been at for years. It didn't say if he was retiring or if he was moving away. He has a stellar reputation, and I know that some of his patients have traveled from across the country to have him as their surgeon. His two specialties are melanoma and breast cancer which are the cancers that I had.

Throughout the years whenever I've had a question, even when it doesn't involve my cancers specifically, if I email him, he responds quickly. A good example of this was when he was lecturing in another country, and I emailed him asking about the cancer dangers of reheating food in certain types of containers. He replied in less than a day.

Yesterday I emailed him at the Medical Center asking him where he was planning to go, and would he still be my doctor.

Today I am happy, relieved, and grateful that he emailed me to say that he would like to continue to see me at his new location, and then he gave me all the details. I am blessed.

May 8th

Today I received a large unexpected envelope in the mail. It was from my cousin, Barbara. Her mom passed away years ago, and she's now taking the time to go through her mom's old photographs. I'm grateful that in the envelope were several photos of my grandfather. I never knew him, and I always wondered what he looked like.

I knew that he was born in Russia but later moved to Paris. At that time Russia wasn't safe for Jews. He later immigrated to America with my grandmother and their three children. One of those youngsters was my dad. At some point he had a good job teaching in a college in the Northeast, but for reasons that I don't know he returned to Russia, abandoning my grandmother and their children. By that time they had five children.

I don't have any warm and fuzzy feelings about my grandfather, but I'm sincerely grateful that Barbara sent me these pictures. Someday I'd like to know the rest of his story.

May 9th

I'm grateful for something that Dave's good friend, Arnold, did for me today. When he found out about the orchid plants that Dave used to give me, he sent me a beautiful orchid wrist corsage. I'm grateful for his kindness and thoughtfulness. I'm even more grateful that he and Dave rekindled their friendship after having not seen each other for decades. Their reunion happened just a few months before Dave passed away when Arnold had a conference in our city.

Carpe Diem.

May 10th

I had a happy Mother's Day dinner on my back porch with Michael, Aaliya, Kathleen, and Aaliya's mom, Sharon. I wore the beautiful wrist corsage that Arnold sent to me.

It was tough not to be able to hug each other, but we wanted to be careful to socially distance. The "kids" fixed a delicious dinner—cheese and crackers, salad, salmon, risotto rice with peas, and lemon cake. And, the mimosas were REALLY good, too. I'd give Chez Browne 5 Stars.

They gave me a four pack of toilet paper as a gift. In this age of COVID-19 it's both a funny and valuable gift.

Today, like all days, I'm grateful and blessed to have the kids that I have.

May 11th

Yesterday's dinner was superb! Today I'm grateful for yummy leftovers!

May 12th

Both Michael and Aaliya work at a hospital. I'm thankful for a text that Aaliya sent me that said that the hospital's 2020 brochure is titled *The Year of the Nurse*. I thought that was a wonderful title for this year of the pandemic.

It made my day to read the part of Aaliya's text that said that Michael's picture is in the brochure.

I'm a proud and grateful mom.

May 13th

Whenever someone has asked me when I was diagnosed with breast cancer, I've always said that it was in 2009. I knew that it was in the summer, but I've long ago forgotten the exact date. It really didn't matter to me.

Today I received a copy of an order from my medical oncologist for a mammogram and an ultrasound that I need to schedule. When I was looking over the order something stood out that I had never noticed before. It listed the date of my diagnosis to be on August 13,

2009. Seeing that date brought tears to my eyes because that's when my battle with cancer began.

Dave passed away on August 13, 2016. That's when his battle with cancer ended.

Throughout our years together we shared a ton of things. I "guess" that I'm grateful that we shared one last thing–a significant date.

May 14th

I'm grateful that Barbara from my phone carrier was exceptionally nice and patient when I called with iCloud questions.

May 15th

The pandemic has confirmed for me that I'm a people person. I sincerely miss seeing my friends and family as often as I used to see them.

Today my friend, Maryellen, came over to my house for a fun visit and lunch. We socially distanced as we enjoyed a delicious takeout meal, and we talked non-stop.

I'm grateful that restaurants still serve takeout, and I'm grateful for my forever friend.

May 16th

This morning I was doing yardwork in my back yard. I'm grateful that I looked into the lake near my dock at the perfect time. That's when I saw a mother duck leading her four tiny babies on a swim. I think that I could feel happy endorphins as I looked at the pretty sight.

May 17th

Today Facebook reminded me of a memory involving our sailboat. The memory was of a day that was both incredibly sad for me and my kids, but at the same time a day that I was grateful for a man named Matt. The following is what I had written on Facebook, not all that long after Dave had passed away:

Over the weekend I said, "Goodbye" to the Sally B, the sailboat that Dave and I bought 30 years ago. Her original name was Moon Shadow, but Dave really wanted to change the name to Sally B. Her new name was painted on the stern, and he registered her with the Coast Guard as Sally B.

It was a tough goodbye for me for two main reasons. The first reason was that I watched the source of so many happy memories being trucked up my street. Another chapter of my life had come to an end.

I'd like to share one of my many memories. Michael was about four or five years old and we were spending the weekend on the boat. Both nights Dave and I commented on how clear and beautiful the sky was, and how we could see so many more stars than we could see from home. We were lulled to sleep those nights with a gentle rocking. The sound of the breeze in the rigging was like a lullaby to Dave.

The following morning while Dave cooked breakfast, Michael and I sat in the cockpit. Out of nowhere a family of dolphins came close to our boat and put on a show just for us. It was at that moment that I looked at my husband and my young son, and thanked God for my wonderful life. I had been blessed with the best husband in the world for me, and we had been blessed with a son.

The second reason I was so sad as our boat went slowly up the street is because of the dreams that will never become a reality. A few years ago Dave trucked our boat from the marina to our house for a massive restoration project. The Sally B is an ocean going vessel, but Dave wanted to be certain that it was in the best shape possible for a sail that he and Kathleen were going to take–they were going to sail to Ireland together. It broke my heart on Saturday to see Kathleen's sadness as she watched our boat be taken away.

Dave had built many of the parts for the boat–the bowsprit, the companionway, hatch covers, and the tiller to name just a few pieces. I'll never forget the day that he walked into the kitchen holding the tiller that he had just finished making. He had a big smile on his face and asked me what I thought. I told him I thought that it was beautiful, and that it looked like a piece of art.

I asked the man who bought our boat if I could keep the tiller. He said, "Yes," and said that he thought that was the perfect part of the boat for me to keep.

The tiller isn't a huge piece, but it's crucial because it steers the boat. In the future, on days that I'm feeling a little down, I can look at the tiller and hope in some way that Dave will help steer me in the right direction. I know that may sound silly, but ... it's me.

Dave had a website that documented his restoration project. Shortly before he passed away, he told me that he was still getting over 1000 hits a month from around the world. I plan on keeping the site active. If you ever want to take a look at it, it's Bristol29.com

Matt, the man who bought our boat, was heaven-sent. When I emailed him that I accepted his offer, he immediately responded by saying he was "humbled, saddened, excited, happy." He also said that when she's back in the water that Michael, Kathleen, and I have a forever invitation to come stay at his house in Georgia with him and his family, and to go sailing with them.

He wrote a comment on Dave's online funeral home guestbook. It said, "David, I never knew you here, but I know that I would have liked you a lot. I look forward to sailing with you."

I am blessed.

May 18th

This may seem like a trifle reason to be grateful, but I sincerely am. We've seldom had a problem with ants in our house, but in the last week or so things have changed. Three days ago I went to a do it yourself pest control store in hopes of buying something to get rid of the problem. I'm happy to say that I haven't seen any ants in my house in the last two days.

May 19th

Even though I'm only cooking for myself these days, I continue to cook the same type of meals that I cooked when we were a family of four, and later when it was just Dave and me.

A recipe that I really enjoy using is for my chicken scaloppini. A key ingredient is cream sherry. Recently, I've only been able to find the large size bottle of cream sherry at my grocery store, even though they continue to carry the smaller bottle of regular sherry. I don't want a big bottle of the cream sherry or a small bottle of regular sherry. I want a small bottle of cream sherry.

Today I took the time to drive to two additional stores. I'm grateful that I found what I was looking for, and for the delicious chicken scaloppini that I cooked for my dinner tonight.

May 20th

It's hot and it's humid outside. For the last four days, it's been pretty hot inside my house, too, because the air conditioner wasn't working. I'm grateful for ceiling fans.

Today I'm even more grateful for air conditioning, and that mine has been repaired.

May 21st

I've been taking Molly with me for a ride in the car whenever I'm dropping something off at the Post Office, or I'm going to my bank's drive-thru lane.

I know that she is super-duper happy for these short excursions.

Today I was grateful that the bank teller put a doggy treat for Molly in the chute, along with my receipt.

May 22nd

Ninetta has been a BFF since we were children in 6th grade. She lives a couple of hours from me, but we talk on a regular basis. Today when she called and asked how I was doing, I started crying and told her that I was "losing it from being in this pandemic lockdown."

We talked for at least an hour. By the time we said, "Goodbye," I was feeling a million times better. That's what a talk with a BFF can do.

I'm grateful for mine.

May 23rd

I never know when Kathleen is going to stop by for a visit, but I'm always happy to see her. When she came by today, it was to show me her haircut. It was really pretty, and considerably shorter–12 inches shorter.

She had donated her hair to Wigs for Kids. This wasn't the first time that she's done this act of kindness.

I had cancer. I lost all my hair. I know how very, very happy Kathleen's donation is going to make a child and her parents feel.

I'm grateful for what my daughter did today.

May 24th

I buy Molly's prescription dog food directly from her veterinarian. Since the pandemic has begun, I call ahead of time to tell them what I want to buy, and I pay for it over the phone. When I arrive to pick it up, I call to let them know that I'm in their parking lot, I open my trunk, and then someone comes out and puts her food into my trunk.

I'm grateful that it's so easy and safe.

May 25th

When I was checking out at the grocery store this afternoon I was a few cents short. I'm grateful that the cashier smiled and said, "Don't worry about it."

I'm grateful for her kindness, and that I didn't have to break another bill and be given change. During COVID- 19 I'm trying to be as cautious as possible.

May 26th

Dave always took care of whatever needed to be done with our well water. Shortly before he passed away he bought two new filter tanks to make sure that our water was safe. One is a sediment filter tank. The other is a carbon filter tank. Additionally, I have the water tested by a State certified lab every year.

The tanks are far from being old, but this is 2020. Need I say more?

The sediment filter tank stopped working, and for reasons too detailed to mention the warranty wasn't honored. For weeks my water has been filtered only by the carbon filter. I have absolutely no knowledge or experience in well water filter tanks, and dealing with this sort of thing really stresses me out. None of my friends or family have a well for their drinking water, so I have nobody that I personally know to help me make wise decisions. Floyd, who helped fix the problem with the leak with one of the well's pressure tanks, does not deal with filter tanks.

So why am I grateful? I'm grateful for an individual by the name of Keanu who is located many states away from me. He works for the company where Dave bought the tank. After many phone conversations, and a lot of texts were exchanged for more than a month between us, I finally bought a new sediment filter tank. Even though the warranty wasn't honored, Keanu sold the new tank to me for half price, and it will be here in a matter of days.

May 27th

I'm grateful and relieved that buying a new filter tank is behind me.

When Dave bought the last two tanks, he and his brother, John, installed them. They knew exactly how it needed to be done. On the other hand, I would need to hire someone who could do that work for me, and I needed to find someone before the new tank would be delivered.

Since I've ordered the tank I've been calling different companies and individuals. Two did not return my calls. Others wanted to sell me water softeners. One came out and looked at the tanks and told me that he didn't like the "new, fancy tanks," and that he had something better for me. I reminded him that I had already purchased a new tank, and that I was just waiting for it to be delivered. I decided that he wasn't the person that I was looking for.

This morning I left a message at another local company. Within an hour Alan called me back and said that he was the owner of the company, and that he'd been in that business for more than 30 years. He asked if he could come to my house and look at the setup of the tanks and how they were plumbed.

I'm grateful that he came to my house this afternoon, and he said that my new tank will be easy to install. He said to call him when the tank is delivered, and that he will be out the same day to install it.

I feel like a weight has been lifted from my shoulders that I've been carrying for more than a month. I'm feeling much gratitude for Alan.

May 28th

Today one of my kids asked me for advice. I'm grateful that even though they're adults, they still value my opinion.

May 29th

I'm grateful that the hair salons are now reopened. I'm also grateful that Cristina opened her salon early this morning, and that she made my appointment the first one of the day. There were no other people in the salon, and both Cristina and I were masked.

I'm grateful for my first haircut in months, and that I felt safe.

May 30th

This morning I felt like I was in a pandemic hole. I was missing what my life was like before the pandemic.

I am grateful that throughout the day, without them even knowing how I felt, I heard from family and friends. The texts that I received from my cousins, Paula and Barbara, and the phone calls from my cousin, Ireland, and my friend, Kim, lifted my spirits.

Even on days that I'm a little down, I know that I am greatly blessed. There are many people living by themselves who didn't hear from anyone today.

May 31st

Hurricane season begins tomorrow. The weather forecasters all say that it's going to be an active hurricane season.

Today the tree service that we've used for years came to my house to make sure that all our large trees look healthy and not about to break a big limb if a hurricane comes our way.

I'm grateful that Shelby said my trees are in good shape. My wallet and my peace of mind are grateful, too.

JUNE

June 1st

Bad news/Good news–My cousin, Paula, called me today. As always, we had a nice chitchat. During our conversation, however, she told me that she had fallen and had been in the hospital, but she was now back at home.

I'm very sorry about her fall and about her hospital stay, but I'm full of gratitude that she's home and feeling much better.

June 2nd

Today I did some maintenance in my home. I put two cups of vinegar into my air conditioning unit, and changed two filters in my refrigerator, and changed the filters in the ceiling for the air conditioner. Adding the vinegar is a nothing burger, but the first few times I had to change the filters it was a bit of a challenge for me. I'm not going to say that the filters are now a piece of cake, but it's definitely getting easier.

I'm grateful to have those things done for a while.

June 3rd

All of our day to day lives have been impacted due to COVID- 19. I sincerely miss interaction with my family and friends, but because we've been encouraged to stay home as much as possible I've been noticing nature more, and those sights make me happy. Perhaps the pandemic has forced me to slow down and see the awesomeness that I've been missing. Here's a snippet of something that happened today:

Each morning I let Molly out on the back porch that's inside the pool's screen enclosure. She barks when she wants to come back inside the house.

Today when she'd been outside for a long time and hadn't barked, I looked out my kitchen window to see what she was up to. She was slowly walking back and forth in a small area. Then she'd stand at attention with her ears perked up, as she watched something moving on the other side of the screen. Whatever she saw wasn't something that caused her to bark. Of course, I wanted to see what she saw.

It was a big turtle intent on doing whatever it is that lake turtles do when they're on land.

Molly continued to watch the turtle, and I continued to watch Molly watching the turtle. I'm grateful to have had this pleasant diversion in my day.

June 4th

I was happy and grateful to see that for a while today, Amazon ranked my long term care book at #133 out of 5000 books in my genre.

June 5th

Today is a date that stands out in my mind. Many years ago on June 5th was the first time that my mom, Dave, and I vacationed together in Ireland. I'm grateful that Facebook reminded me of a wonderful memory that I posted a few years ago. To go along with the post there was also a picture of a young Dave and me enjoying an evening together. Here's what my post said:

This picture was taken during our first vacation to Ireland. We were enjoying a fantastic meal at Maam Cross in Connemara while my mother visited with her two sisters that she hadn't seen in more than 30 years. Mag, and Kate, and my mom enjoyed a happy evening filled with lots of laughter and the best crack they had in a long time. (To my law enforcement friends, it's not what you think.)

Earlier in the day Dave and I had driven past a field full of haystacks. The background was striking, and Dave thought that if we went back there at sunset it would make for a great picture. The summer days in Ireland are long, and the sun doesn't set until around 10:00 at night. So after our dinner was over we drove for nearly an hour to get to that field. The lighting was perfect, and he took lots of pictures.

The ride back to my Aunt Mag's house was memorable as we drove in the pitch dark on the "wrong side" of small windy roads over mountain passes, with the steering wheel on the right side of the car and the stick shift on Dave's left side. As he avoided the occasional sheep that darted in front of our car and the donkey that stood in the road, I silently prayed that he hadn't drunk too many Guinnesses earlier in the evening.

When we got back to Mag's house and told them why we were so late, Mag joked with Dave and told him that we didn't have to drive so far to get a picture of a haystack.

Dave took hundreds (maybe thousands) of pictures of all sorts of things on that trip. To this day, we still have a large framed picture of a haystack hanging in our guest bedroom. However, it's not one of the pictures that he took that night after our dinner at Maam Cross. It's one that he took on Mag's scenic land.

On that first vacation to Ireland Dave fell in love with my many relatives, and also with Ireland. His grandfather was born on the Emerald Isle which allowed Dave to apply for dual citizenship. He proudly framed the formal document that he received from the Irish government. Throughout the years, based on that document, he told me that he was more Irish than I was.

I lovingly always disagreed.

June 6th

I'm grateful that I am safe from the two tornadoes that touched down this evening not far from my neighborhood. I watched the news and weather reports for hours with bated breath. I have to admit that I was scared. Molly was scared, too.

June 7th

Ontavius has been one of Michael's forever friends for a long, long time. When they were seniors in high school Ontavius' family moved to the other side of town which took him out of our school district. It was a no-brainer that he would live with us so that he could continue going to the same school.

Ever since that time he called Dave "Dad," and me "Mom," and Kathleen "Sister," and John "Uncle." I refer to him as my second son. When he got married Michael was in his wedding. Dave, Kathleen, and I were honored to be seated at the table reserved for the immediate family.

I'm always grateful for Ontavius, and I'm thankful that he checked on me today to make sure that I was safe from yesterday's bad weather.

June 8th

Today while I was driving I saw a squirrel run in front of the car in front of me. I was quite sure that it didn't make it. Sometimes, it's a blessing to be wrong. The squirrel made it across the street just fine.

He and I are both grateful.

June 9th

I'm grateful that today I got to see two otters swimming around my dock, and then sunning on it. I noticed the larger one chomping on something. He was a noisy eater, and I could hear him cracking whatever he was eating with his giant teeth.

I watched them both get up at the same time and slide off the dock into the lake. It made me smile when I saw them swim away together, and I remembered that otters usually mate for life.

Watching nature is so much more enjoyable than watching the news these days. I was blessed to have had this opportunity.

June 10th

Today is the anniversary of Dave's and my first date. Throughout the years we celebrated our dating anniversary as much as we did our wedding anniversary. I am so very grateful that long ago Dave had the good sense to have asked me out.

All day today I not only thought about that wonderful first date, but thoughts of our relationship when it was still new kept coming to mind. Sometimes, it's hard to put random thoughts into words, but I'll do my best.

I'm not going to say that it was love at first sight, but there was a definite spark. We saw each other often because of our respective jobs. He was a reporter for a local radio station and covered news stories that involved local politics, law enforcement, and the courts. I worked at the State Attorney's Office.

He was a really good reporter. Well actually, he was a great reporter, and he often broke stories that other radio, TV, and newspaper reporters followed up on. He was so good that on more than one occasion I was called to Administration because they thought that I was the source of leaks. How else could he have known about some of those stories?

Nothing could have been further from the truth–he was just a great reporter. (When I listen to the nightly news and I hear stories about government leaks, it makes me smile to think that once upon a time, I was thought of as a likely leak.)

It took months before he finally asked me out–best date ever. And as the saying goes "the rest is history." I'm not sure when during our two and a half year courtship love came into the relationship. However, I do remember the first time he told me that he loved me.

He was dropping me off in front of the State Attorney's Office after a lunch date. He got out of the car, and then he went around the car to open up my door. That's when he said those three great words–"I love you."

My response was "thank you."

As I rode the empty elevator to my 6th floor office I was shaking my head thinking what a nerd I was. I hoped that he thought that my "thank you" was in response to him opening my door, and not what I thought about his ILY. Actually, I hoped that he hadn't heard what I said at all.

It took quite a while before he said, "I love you" a second time. I didn't say "thank you" that time.

June 11th

Dave was a great barbecuer–seafood, steaks, ribs, veggies, you name it. I'm grateful for all the scrumptious meals that he made on the grill, but I'm seriously missing the taste and the aroma of his delicious grilling.

Today I posted something on Facebook about my gas barbecue grill, and I mentioned that I didn't know how to use it. Bob, one of my friends since my college days, replied to my post by saying that he would teach me how to use it.

I'm grateful for Bob's friendship, and for his kindness, and for the possibility of barbecuing some of my meals.

June 12th

I'm grateful that I have a sense of humor, and that I can laugh at myself. That's a good thing because there have been numerous times in my life that I've committed faux pas.

A handful of my friends have told me that they've been a little down in the dumps during the pandemic. Recently, an idea occurred to me. I thought that if I occasionally post some of my faux pas on Facebook that perhaps it might give some of my friends a reason to laugh, or at least to crack a smile. Here's an example of something that I posted:

When I lived at home with my parents I seldom cooked. The only thing that I remember making were chocolate chip cookies. When I moved into my first apartment I had to cook if I wanted to eat. There were a lot of cooking experiments going on, and sometimes a boyfriend would get to eat what I had cooked. Dave was one of them, and even though he saw some pretty goofy cooking mistakes, I'm blessed that he still wanted to spend a lifetime with me.

I remember I invited him to come over for a dinner of Hungarian Goulash. I followed the recipe step by step, and it was really tasty. He agreed, but somewhere during the dinner he said, "Honey, you know this isn't Hungarian Goulash, don't you?"

"What? Yes, it is," I said, getting my cookbook to prove it. Dang, he was right. I had cooked Beef Stroganoff.

Then there was the time that I had gotten a really good recipe from a co-worker. I followed that recipe exactly, too. It was simple–brown ground beef, add chili powder, followed by cream cheese. Open a can of refrigerated crescent rolls and put a scoop of the mixture on each roll, and then roll them up.

The directions also said that before baking, rub each roll with an egg to give it a nice golden shiny color. I stood at my kitchen counter and methodically rubbed each roll with an egg, making sure that it touched on every part of the rolls. I wanted them to look delicious.

They tasted really good, but I didn't see what difference the egg made. While we were eating I asked Dave if there was a chemical in the eggshell that was supposed to give them a golden shine.

"Honey, what did you do?" he asked.

"I rubbed each one with an egg just like the recipe said to do."

I can still remember him laughing so hard that there were tears coming down his cheeks. Then he got up from his chair and gave me a big hug, and told me that he loved me.

From that evening on, whenever we had crescent rolls we'd often look at each other and smile. We both knew what that smile meant.

June 13th

I'm grateful for the boxes of "gems" that John found in my attic the last time he visited. That visit was shortly before the pandemic had begun.

Today I became a bit sentimental when I read something in one of those boxes. It was written in 1915 by Grandfather Browne, who I've been told was a writer and an inventor. It was titled, "The Things We Ought Not to Have Done" by D.H. Browne.

As I read his words I felt a sense of closeness to my grandfather-in-law, a man I never met. The first paragraph reads:

"There are in the Irish language a great many witty proverbs, some of which you seldom hear in their English translation. One of these relating to widows and old maids will be appreciated. 'It's a lonesome washing,' says the proverb, 'that hasn't a man's shirt in it.'"

At first I laughed when I read it. When I read it a second time I thought that it was a little sexist. But, the more I thought about it, there's actually some truth in that proverb.

Grandfather Browne died in the 1918 pandemic, but today as I read his words I feel like he was speaking to me.

June 14th

Today I came across a handful of email messages between Matt, the man who bought our sailboat, and me. They were from about six months after he became the new owner. I knew that at some point I'd be receiving the type of email that he sent me, but knowing that they would be coming didn't make them any easier to read.

He was asking for my blessing to rename the Sally B to Kate, after his daughter. In that email he said that he and Kate would be honored if I'd also let them refer to s/v Kate as goddaughter to s/v Sally B.

I responded by telling him that I knew from the day that the Sally B left our driveway that she was going to the right home. I knew that her name would be changed, and she would be starting a new life. I told him that Kate was the perfect name for her, and that long before Kathleen was born Dave and I decided that if we ever had a little girl that we wanted to name her Kathleen, and that her nickname would be Kate. We called her Kate for a while, but eventually it seemed that she was more like a Kathleen. Throughout the years, however, Dave, John, and sometimes Michael called her Katie Bug.

Matt quickly emailed me back to say that he calls his daughter Katie Bug more than he calls her Kate. We both had goosebumps. His last email to me that day said, "I think that God and Dave are smiling."

I'm grateful that Matt is the person who now owns our Sally B.

June 15th

I saw a picture today that I had posted on Facebook of Dave, Kathleen, Michael, and me the last time we went to Ireland. My eyes were immediately drawn to Dave's arm around me. I scrolled way up and way down to look at more pictures. In every picture of the two of us together he had his arm around me, or he was holding my hand, or he had his hand on my shoulder.

I sure miss his touch, but I'll be forever grateful for all the years that I had it.

June 16th

Today when I paid my electric bill by phone, I was reminded how grateful I am during the pandemic for things that shouldn't be taken for granted.

The representative asked me a question that I had never been asked before. She asked if my payment was a one-time payment. I told her that I didn't understand her question. She explained that during the pandemic with so many people out of work, the electric company has set up payment plans for those who need it, and her question was asking if I was one of those customers.

When the call was over I was grateful that I was able to pay the entire amount at one time, and I said a prayer for those who can't.

June 17th

Not a day goes by that I don't think of Dave. Earlier today when I was washing my windows I thought how grateful I am that we were both hard workers. I don't think either of us ever said that something was too hard to do, or that a particular job was beneath us.

That got me thinking of when we were newlyweds. We both had good jobs, but we were young and didn't make much money. We were also trying our hardest to save what we could for a down payment on our first home.

So together we took a second job in the evenings and on the weekends when we weren't working at our "real jobs." We worked seven days a week as janitors at a large car dealership. It was hard, yucky work, but we stayed focused on our goal–a down payment for a home to call our own.

I'm grateful that we were a team in this endeavor that lasted for several months, and that Dave was always the one who cleaned the bathrooms.

June 18th

I'm really grateful that we had Bunco tonight!

Well, we didn't actually have Bunco–we didn't play the game, or eat the good food, or hug each other, but through Zoom we got to see each other, and smile at each other, and talk to each other, and be as close as we could be to each other, without really being together.

Aww, the wonders of technology.

June 19th

Today I heard a discussion of Jim Croce's hit song from long ago, "If I Could Save Time in a Bottle."

I've always thought the words to that song were beautiful. Where I am at this point in my life, particularly during these unprecedented pandemic times, the words are even more meaningful to me than ever before.

We all know that time can't be saved, but I'm extremely grateful that throughout my life I've been blessed to have made wonderful memories with the people that I love most. I'm thankful that those memories are saved in my mind.

June 20th

I was pleasantly surprised that when I looked at Facebook today, I saw an incredibly nice comment about me written by Stephen, a co-worker from a long time ago. April, another colleague, quickly followed up Stephen's comment by saying, "I agree."

I'm grateful that my former co-workers remember our time working together for the good of our community, and shared their sweet memory of me for others to see.

June 21st

Today is Father's Day. It's a bittersweet day for me, however, because all the fathers who were in my life, who loved me and I loved, have all passed away. But, I'm going to try hard to focus on the sweet.

I was blessed and our children were blessed that Dave was such a wonderful father.

I was blessed that I had a loving father, even though he didn't have a great role model as a father.

I was blessed that my father-in-law, Roland, loved me as if I was his own daughter, and he often told me that I was the daughter that he never had.

I was blessed that my Uncle Colman, who was also my godfather, was a man that I deeply loved, and who loved me, too.

Even though they are all gone, I'm so very grateful that God blessed me with each of them for a while along my life's journey.

I'm also grateful that Dave helped to raise such a thoughtful son. Michael and Aaliya knew that today was probably going to be a little melancholy for me, so they called to tell me that they love me.

67

June 22nd

Today when I was watering my indoor plants I thought of my Aunt Delia. I have so many loving memories of her that those memories could easily fill a book. I'll be forever grateful that she was my aunt and my godmother, but today I'm also grateful for her healthy flowering plants.

She had two beautiful African violet plants. After she went into a nursing home I continued to take care of her, and I tried my best to take care of her plants, too. Unlike my aunt, I don't have a green thumb, and one of her plants died. Since then I've been working hard to keep the other one healthy. It's more than 40 years old.

Two years ago I cut six leaves from the elderly plant, and planted each leaf in its own small plastic cup. All of those leaves sprouted additional leaves. I've since repotted the new plants that had started in the small cups, into larger pots. All six new plants that came from Aunt Delia's 40 year old plant are now flowering beautifully.

Today when I noticed how pretty the baby African violet plants have become, and how healthy and flowering the old one still is, I was really grateful that my thumb is perhaps a bit greener than I thought. I think that Aunt Delia would be grateful, too.

June 23rd

I bought a new pair of badly needed running shoes today. I am grateful to Bruce, the salesman, who gave me a 10% discount.

June 24th

I watched an oldie goldie movie tonight–*Murphy's Romance*. It's a rom-com that Dave and I saw in a theater way back in the mid-80s.

I'm grateful for tonight's enjoyable entertainment as well as a memory of a romantic date night.

June 25th

This evening I thanked God for the beautiful view from my back yard–big, fluffy, white and pink and grey clouds against a bright blue sky were all reflecting on the lake.

I'm grateful how much looking at that view lifted my spirits.

June 26th

Today Facebook posted one of Dave's memories which brought me back to a happy moment in time. The post said, "Eating dinner with my love, Sally Browne."

When he posted that restaurant check-in a few years ago, I thought that it was sweet. Today I got misty eyed when I read that he referred to me as his love.

Grateful, grateful, grateful for our years together.

June 27th

Today as the livestreamed Mass was coming to an end, it dawned on me that I have a huge gift to be thankful for that I never realized I had been given.

My mom was a devout Catholic. My dad was Jewish. This could have been a huge problem, a house divided, but it never was. My mom often went to the synagogue with my dad on Friday nights and on Saturday mornings. My dad often attended Mass with my mom and me on Sundays.

Now that I'm older and a bit wiser, I'm grateful for the respect my parents had for each other and for each other's religion.

June 28th

I'm grateful for the supper I had tonight.

I had fresh salmon, potatoes, mushrooms, coleslaw, and sautéed spinach with raisins. My plate was laden with leftovers from meals that I'd cooked over the last few days. It may not sound like everything would go well together, but they did.

My mom would have called the meal a mongaray. I don't know if that's a Gaelic word or just a word that she made up. She said that it meant "a little of this and a little of that."

Dave used to love our mongaray meals. He would have loved this one, too.

June 29th

I'm grateful for something that happens every day that I have yet to mention. Each day my friend, Theresa, texts me with encouraging words.

A recent text said, "God is breathing new life into old ideas."

I don't have a clue what that could be, but I'm grateful for the possibilities.

June 30th

Robert is the son of one of my BFFs. He's only 37 years old, and has been battling leukemia for more than three and a half years. Over the last several months he's been awfully sick. He's been septic, and in and out of the ICU. However, today is a day to rejoice because he was well enough and strong enough to have a stem cell transplant. The stem cells were donated by his sister, Sarah.

There are no words to express how grateful I am for this wonderful update that his mom shared with me.

JULY

July 1st

April 15th wasn't when our income taxes were due this year. Due to the pandemic, the date was extended to July 15th. My payment is now on its way to Uncle Sam.

I'm grateful that the date was extended, and I'm also grateful that I don't have to think about it for another year.

July 2nd

My cousin, Rose, is a clown.

I'm not joking. She really is a clown who has a natural ability to make people feel good and to laugh. She's turned this talent into an avocation.

I'm grateful for Rose, and that she invited me to the Bump a Nose and Clown Around Zoom meeting today to learn more about Caring Clowning.

July 3rd

Earlier today I sent a text to Kathleen that said, "I'm glad that you're my daughter. I love you."

She texted back, "I'm glad you're my mom. I love you, too."

I'm grateful and blessed to read those words.

July 4th

Many of my friends have experienced the 4th of July at the Brownes. I say this with as much humility as possible–it was always a fun time!

We watched our kids grow up together. In the early years the girls hung out with the girls, and the boys hung out with the boys. As the years went by, the two groups hung out together. They spent a lot of time in the pool, but when they got older Dave took anyone for a ride in our motor boat who wanted to go for a ride. A big hit was when he took them tubing behind the boat.

The food was always delicious, as each family brought a dish to share–calico beans, homemade coleslaw, ribs, thin mint pie, to name just a few of the goodies. Dave barbecued the hot dogs and burgers.

Thanks to many of the neighbors who lived around the lake, the evening was always topped off with a fireworks display that was second to none. There were so many fireworks going off at the same time that it was difficult to know which direction you should be looking. One year, thanks to the awesome photography of our friend, Joe, a picture of the fireworks that he took from our yard landed on the front page of our local newspaper.

The 4th of July has changed dramatically since Dave passed away. There haven't been any more 4th of July parties at our house, but tonight with Kathleen, Michael, and Aaliya watching the fireworks at my house with me, there was no place on Earth I'd rather be.

I'm so grateful for my kids.

July 5th

My cousins aren't just family, they're also my friends.

I'm happy and I'm grateful that my cousin, Josie, called me today from Ireland. It was great hearing her voice, and catching up with what's been happening with each other during the pandemic.

July 6th

One of Kathleen's close friends tested positive for COVID- 19. I pray that she gets well soon.

I'm grateful and relieved that Kathleen's test came back negative.

July 7th

I'm grateful that my nose wasn't stuffy today. That may not seem like a reason to be in a gratitude journal, but during allergy season it really is.

July 8th

I took an online defensive driving class today. It was easy peasy. I'm grateful that those few hours the class took to complete will save additional money on my car insurance.

July 9th

When I was two and a half years old, my mom wanted to "go home" for a visit to Ireland. I still have vivid memories of the months that we spent at my Aunt Kate's and Uncle Colman's house. Of course, those memories in my mind's eye are those made by a child–riding on donkeys, playing with dogs, and being down by the sea with my cousins.

One of those cousins was Bobbie. When Mom and I returned to America and to my dad, Bobbie was with us. She was only 16 years old, and our house and America became her new home.

Bobbie and I have been close throughout our lives, even though we no longer live near each other and don't get to see each other very often.

I'm so grateful that she called me today, and that we had a long talk. I'll always be grateful for our strong bond.

July 10th

Today I was glancing over the first book that I wrote, and when I read the book's Acknowledgements I thought of my friend, Brendan. My thoughts went beyond the help that he gave me for my book.

He is another person that I've known since high school. He wasn't a classmate; he was a teacher. Throughout the years our paths have crossed many times. Lucky for me that somewhere along the way he went from being an acquaintance to being a friend.

He and my Aunt Delia were also friends. He, too, was born in Ireland. Months before my aunt's 100th birthday, he shared information with me about Ireland that I never knew. He explained the Centenarian Bounty to me. It's an Irish government program that benefits anyone on their 100th birthday who was born in Ireland but who no longer lives there.

Delia was born in Ireland, but she lived most of her life in America. Brendan explained that through this program she was eligible to be sent a generous check as a 100th birthday present. He explained what documents I would need to gather to send to the Irish government in order for this to happen.

I followed the steps that Brendan told me to do, and on Delia's 100th birthday she received this wonderful gift from Ireland. She was grateful and thrilled to receive it. She was also sincerely thankful to Brendan and to me.

I will be forever grateful to Brendan for sharing this information with me, for walking me through the process, and for putting a huge smile on my aunt's face.

July 11th

I never had the good fortune of knowing my mother-in-law. That's because she and my father-in-law were involved in a car accident a few years before I met Dave. They were driving to the library in downtown when a car going north crossed over the center lane and ran head-on into their southbound car. There were no other cars nearby, nor was there an explanation why the other driver did what he did. My father-in-law was severely injured and my mother-in-law died as a result of the accident.

Over the years Dave would occasionally say that if just one thing had been different that morning, the accident wouldn't have occurred. If his parents couldn't find the car keys, or if they had slept a few more minutes, or if they had stopped for gas, or if...

This morning I had a meeting in downtown. When I got into my car I remembered something that I needed for the meeting that I had left in the house. I went back inside and got it. When I got into the car a second time I remembered something else I needed, so back into the house I went again. When I got into the car for a third time and put the key into the ignition, it wouldn't turn. I don't mean that the engine wouldn't turn on. I mean the key wouldn't turn. Today was the first time that's happened.

After about a minute of trying to get it to turn, it worked just fine and I was on my way to the meeting. My route was the same one I've taken thousands of times before, and I drove past where my in-laws had their accident. Later this evening I remembered the conversations with Dave about if one thing had been different the morning his mom was killed that she wouldn't have been involved in the accident. I wonder if the way my morning started out had absolutely no meaning, or if maybe this was Divine Intervention.

I gratefully think the latter.

July 12th

My wonderful neighbor, Cathy, brought me homemade cupcakes this evening for absolutely no reason. I'm blessed that she's my neighbor, and I'm so grateful that for the next few nights I'll have delicious bedtime snacks.

July 13th

There was a bit of an explosion in my kitchen today. It was startling enough that it caused Molly to quickly leave the room with her tail between her legs. It caused me to scream, and I think my heart skipped a beat or two. This is what happened:

I had just returned home from the store and had brought all the bags of groceries into the house and had placed them on the counter. As I was taking the items out of the bags I heard a very loud pop coming from a bag on the other side of the kitchen.

I'm not sure why it happened, but a can of refrigerated rolls had popped open on its own.

I never realized until today just how loud that sound is. I also think that pandemic life is perhaps making me a little jumpy.

I'm grateful this evening that a can of dough was the cause of my scream, and that it wasn't something truly sinister.

July 14th

The dentist is never a destination that I would call fun, but it's routinely important. When I visited the dentist's office today for a cleaning with the hygienist and a checkup with the doctor, they did an oral cancer screening.

I'm grateful and relieved that the dentist said everything looked normal.

July 15th

My cousin, Ireland, sent me a YouTube video about "The 7 Things to Do for a Happy Life." I thought that it was really motivating. I also thought it was good to hear that I'm doing the things they recommend doing.

I'm grateful that Ireland sent the video to me. I'm also grateful that I'm happy most of the time.

July 16th

I'm grateful for another of my BFFs—Mary.

We've been friends since we were barely teenagers. We've shared some of life's best of times together as well as some of our worst of times. Mary is now going through a terrible time in her life.

I have some upcoming doctors' appointments that I'm concerned about, so I texted her to ask if she would please say a prayer for me. As soon as I asked I thought how selfish I was for asking her for anything, in light of all that she's going through. I texted her a second time and apologized for my earlier text.

My eyes filled with tears when she texted back and said, "You are perhaps the least selfish person I know," and then she asked about my doctors' appointments.

I'm so grateful for Mary's kind words, and that she's a forever friend.

July 17th

I'm grateful that Kathleen visited me today, and that she gave Molly a bath. I'm not sure how grateful Molly is.

July 18th

This morning as I ate my breakfast I glanced over at the calendar hanging on the kitchen wall. Each month has a different picture that I picked from some of my favorite memories. The picture that's displayed for July was taken many years ago of Dave and me in Ashford Castle in Ireland.

This particular picture brought back fond memories of freelance work we did together when we'd vacation in Ireland. We were a team.

I wrote travel articles about Ireland, and Dave was the photographer. I got the byline, and he got credit for the photography for our articles that appeared in newspapers across the U.S. We did this for several years.

I'm so grateful for the fun times we had and the memories we made on those adventures when we took vacations from our "real jobs."

July 19th

I'm grateful for the birds that sing so lovely each morning. When I took Molly outside early today, their beautiful voices seemed much more noticeable to me than usual. I was surprised that the one with the prettiest sounds of all was the smallest of them all.

The hawks, and the crows, and the ducks, and other waterbirds may not have been singing, but they all had a lot to say to each other. Even the squirrels were chatty this morning.

It was a wonderful way to start my day.

July 20th

Today when I went to the grocery store I had a hard time getting a shopping cart. They were all stuck together. I tried separating the carts at the beginning of the line and at the end of the line, but I couldn't get one to budge.

That's when a polite twentysomething walked into the store and stopped to help me get a cart. I thanked him and asked him his name. I told him he was going on my gratitude list for today.

He said, "Thank you kindly. My name is Jeff."

I'm grateful for Jeff, and that total strangers still do random acts of kindness.

July 21st

I'm grateful that this morning I was able to handle a problem by myself. A few years ago when Dave was alive, I can't imagine being able to do it. Now, I have no choice.

I have a little "thing" going on with one of my eyes, so I can't see great at the moment. When I was standing at my kitchen window I noticed something hanging from one of my gutters inside the pool enclosure. I thought it was a leaf. The operative word is "enclosure." I should be separated from creepy, crawly, slithery things outside the enclosure, right?

Well, that's not how it is in my world these days. These creepy things have somehow figured out a way to get inside the enclosure and visit me. Recently, there was a snake out there. I don't know how it got in or out, but I was afraid to go out there for several days after I saw it.

This morning I had another visitor. When I went outside to look at the leaf that was hanging from my gutter I realized that it wasn't a leaf. I got within inches of this thing that turned its beady eyes and looked at me. It was a baby bat. I could have so easily freaked out but I stayed surprisingly calm as I dealt with batboy. I didn't want to hurt him so I gently nudged him with a broom in hopes that he'd fly out the screen door that I left open to the back yard for his exit.

My efforts to remove him probably looked comical. With each nudge he'd fly from where he was nudged; I'd scream as he zipped past me; Molly would bark from inside the house when she heard me scream; and the bat would fly back and attach to the screen a little higher. This happened three times before I was able to get him to leave my screen enclosure, and to close the door behind him.

I'm grateful that I was able to muster the nerve to do what needed to be done. I pray that I won't have to do it ever again.

July 22nd

The lake is always so pretty on a sunny morning. Today the light was just right and the lake looked like it had sparkly diamonds moving across it with the water's flow.

After yesterday's encounter with batboy, I was grateful for this beautiful gift today.

July 23rd

I had a mammogram and an ultrasound today. I was grateful when the technician told me that the radiologist said that everything looked normal. As a breast cancer survivor I'm always a little nervous before the tests, and I always breathe a sigh of relief to hear that all is well.

Just as I got back into my car, I received a call from my dermatologist's office. Good news, but not great news.

The nurse was calling about yesterday's regularly scheduled checkup. Since there were a few odd looking bumps right on top of my melanoma scar, and a few more right next to it, the doctor did biopsies.

I was grateful that the nurse was calling to say that the biopsy results were negative. However, there were precancerous cells detected on the melanoma scar. She said that when I return next week to have the stitches taken out, the doctor will freeze the precancerous area.

I'm so grateful that it was found before it turned into cancer.

July 24th

I recently received an email that I wasn't sure was from the sender it said it was from. It said that it was from the company that maintains the Domain Name for my first book's website. The email appeared to be legit, although it was a bit pushy and was looking for a payment that wasn't due at this time.

I forwarded the email to our friend, Joe, and told him my concern. He's the person who created the beautiful website. He responded by saying that it was a phishing email and a total scam, and that I had nothing to worry about.

I'm grateful that Joe quickly reassured me that the Domain Name is safe (sandwichedboomer.com) and I'm grateful that tonight I'll sleep well because of his reassurance.

July 25th

My homeowner's insurance premium for my home was reduced considerably because of the new roof, and because of the wind mitigation inspection. I'm gratefully stunned.

July 26th

I was Kathleen's transportation today so that she could have car maintenance done. When I picked her up at the car dealership early this morning, I think she was surprised and grateful that I had brought her some homemade eggplant and a brownie for her lunch later in the day at her office.

I was equally surprised and grateful that she'd brought me an iced coffee. Life is good.

July 27th

I'm overflowing with gratitude that Robert got out of the hospital today after having had a stem cell transplant nearly a month ago. This is the best news I've heard in a long, long time!

He rang the bell!!!

July 28th

I can never see too many rainbows. I'm grateful for the beautiful double rainbow I saw from my back yard today.

July 29th

I went back to the dermatologist today to have the stitches removed from my shin, and to have that area frozen because of the precancerous cells.

The nurse removed the stitches. When the doctor entered the room with a canister of liquid nitrogen in his hand, he immediately said the area where the stitches were removed was too red to freeze today. He said that's an area that is prone to developing ulcers. He told me to come back in two weeks and that he'd freeze the area at that time.

I'm a little concerned because that is exactly the area that my aunt developed an ulcer after having had skin cancer treatment. It was a huge problem that she had for nearly seven years, and there was even a time or two that amputation was discussed. I'm grateful that when she passed away, even though she still had the egregious looking ulcer, she had both her legs.

I'm also extremely grateful that my doctor is being cautious in caring for my leg.

July 30th

Today I was doing some exercises on my bedroom floor. I was stretched out, my eyes were closed, and I thought that I was alone.

Nope. When I opened my eyes I saw that I had a visitor quietly stretched out next to me. It was Molly.

If there is such a thing as a dog loving their human, I know that she loves me. I also know that I love her, and I am so grateful that she's mine.

July 31st

My refrigerator is covered with magnets that are souvenirs from places that we've been. This morning when I was grabbing something out of the fridge, the magnet from Key West caught my attention. A few minutes later when I was sitting at my kitchen counter, sipping my coffee, I daydreamed about some of our vacations in the Florida Keys. It was one of our first vacations as newlyweds, and it was one of our last vacations as a family.

We snorkeled, and fished, and sailed, and motorboated. We ate at No Name Pizza that was located on No Name Key. We sometimes parked on the side of the road and watched the key deer as they roamed wild. Sometimes, we'd get out of the car and they'd let us get close enough to pet them before they ran back into the woods. There were times that we tried to get a little "culture" in Key West so we visited Hemingway's house. We drove on the old two-lane 7 Mile Bridge, as well as on the new multilane one. The old bridge always gave me sweaty palms if I was driving.

The sunsets were phenomenal, and no matter how many times we watched the sun set we marveled at the beauty of each and every one of them. Sharing that view with Dave and my kids was the icing on the cake.

It really didn't matter to me what we did in the Keys. That's because the best part of each of those vacations was just hanging out with the people I loved most.

I'm so grateful to have these memories.

AUGUST

August 1st

This morning as I turned the calendar to August I knew that this month had some milestone anniversaries. This was the month that I was diagnosed with breast cancer. In my mind's eye I pictured Dave and me sitting side by side as the radiologist asked if we wanted to hear the good news or the bad news first. I told her that I'd like to get the bad news out of the way.

She said that I had an aggressive breast cancer. She showed us my mammogram from the prior week and pointed out the tumor. Then she showed us the mammogram from eight months earlier. She pointed out that same tumor, and she said that it was missed when that mammogram was read. Dave was holding my hand and gave it a squeeze.

Then she gave us the good news. She said that until she got the results of the biopsy that she was concerned that my melanoma had spread to my breast, and that would have been more difficult to cure than breast cancer.

Today as I think back to that scary day, there are no words to describe how grateful and blessed I am that Dave was with me every step of the way with my battle with cancer, and that the melanoma had not metastasized.

I'm blessed that with the help of God, and with Dave's help, I made it through this hell of a journey that was about to begin.

August 2nd

I called my plumber, Jim, to please come to my house when he had a chance. I told him that it wasn't an emergency, at least not yet. I'd been hearing a funky sound in the ceiling over the bathtub whenever I flushed the toilet, and I was concerned that there may be a problem with a pipe.

Jim came to my house today and went into the attic to investigate. When he came down he told me that everything looked fine, even though he didn't know what was causing the noise. I'm grateful for that good news.

When I asked him what I owed him, he said that he wasn't charging me anything. He told me to do something with the money to help someone else. He said if everyone did what he was suggesting that we'd live in a better world.

I'm grateful for Jim's kindness, and for his words of wisdom.

August 3rd

The last few evenings when I've written in my gratitude journal I started thinking, *What if? What if I turned my journal into a book?*

I have so much to be grateful for every day, even during a pandemic. Something tells me that we all do. My gratefulness often stems from the obvious good things that have happened during the day. Other times I'm grateful for a wonderful memory of something that once brought me much happiness. Either way, there is always something each day that causes me to feel gratitude.

Today I'm grateful for this idea of a gratitude book.

August 4th

I'm grateful that I learned how to do something new today, thanks to my neighbor, George.

I had an electrical issue at my house that caused a problem first thing this morning. George is an electrician and when I texted him what was happening, he told me to reset the GFI. I didn't have a clue what a GFI is, let alone how to reset it.

He explained what I needed to do, which turned out to be an easy fix to the problem, even for me.

August 5th

From the time I was a child, my bedtime snack was usually three cookies that I dunked into a glass of cold milk. This practice continued in my life long after Dave and I were married. Somewhere along the way, however, I gave up cookies forever. As unlikely as this may sound, I don't remember the specific reason why.

I do remember that there were times in my life when a major problem could have ended terribly. Whenever I faced that sort of problem I prayed that things would turn out okay. It was during one of those times that I offered to never eat another cookie for as long as I live, in gratitude for answered prayers. There were enough of those problems over the years that the angst that they caused me sometimes blends them together in my mind. I don't think that I will ever remember which one was the reason I gave up cookies.

Throughout the years whenever Dave offered me cookie dough ice cream, which the rest of the family loved, I always said, "No, thank you," and told him that cookie dough was sort of like an unborn cookie.

Michael would occasionally tell me that Jesus doesn't care if I eat a cookie. My answer always was that whether or not He cares, a promise is a promise, and I won't ever eat another cookie.

To this day, I still bake awesome chocolate chip cookies and share them with my friends. I just don't eat them myself.

Today I'm sincerely grateful for all answered prayers, even though I may not remember what all those prayers were for.

August 6th

Yesterday evening I needed to call the air conditioning repairman for one of our tenants. I hoped that he would be able to come soon because the weather has been scorching. I also hoped that it wouldn't be difficult to fix the problem.

I'm grateful that the repairman went to their house early today, figured the problem out quickly, and completed the job before noon. I always want our tenants to be comfortable. I'm grateful for them, too.

August 7th

On my morning walk I came across a beautiful big white egret standing on the weir a few blocks from my house. It was a stunning sight with the blue sky and fluffy clouds reflecting on the water right by the little waterfall. I had my phone with me so I took a picture.

The picture was so pretty that I sent it to one of the local weathermen. He responded almost immediately and asked if he could share the picture on social media. Of course, I said, "Yes."

He tweeted the picture and gave me credit for taking it. It was later retweeted by a few people.

I'm grateful that I got to see that beautiful bird. I'm also grateful that the weatherman thought my picture was good enough to share with his viewers. What a lovely way to start a new day!

August 8th

Today I was embarrassed and sorry for something that I had done. However, I still had a reason to be grateful.

I was in a big box store to buy some light bulbs. Just as I picked up a large box of them, it seemed like the store got quiet. That helped anyone near the bulb aisle to hear the loud sound of breaking glass when I accidently dropped the box.

Three employees appeared almost immediately, one with a broom. I kept apologizing, but they kept saying that it was okay and not to worry about it. One of them said that it happens all the time.

I doubt that's true, but I sincerely appreciated that they were trying to make me feel better about my butterfingers.

Today I'm grateful for those three employees and the kindness they showed me.

August 9th

I'm grateful to Stacy at Amazon. She has worked diligently for almost a week in order to get information for me in reference to my first book. The info she was researching didn't have an easy answer, and I sincerely appreciate all that she did to help me.

August 10th

There was a goofy bird sitting at the end of my dock this morning doing what looked a lot like stretching exercises. She stretched her long neck high towards the sky, then slowly to the left, and then to the right. She also stretched her wings towards her back. I watched as she did her stretches several times.

I was sorry that I didn't have my phone nearby to video what she was doing. It would have been cute to watch again, along with the music of "Sittin' on the Dock of the Bay."

I'm grateful that I got to watch this bird's morning routine.

August 11th

Grateful to have heard these words today, "Mom, you're so smart."

August 12th

Today I had my follow-up appointment with the dermatologist to freeze the precancerous cells found on my melanoma scar. Once again, the doctor felt that the area was too red to freeze, and that I would risk developing an ulcer if he froze it today.

The procedure has been rescheduled for another two weeks. He said that he would freeze it at that time, even if it is still red. Of course, I'm a little anxious, but at the same time I'm grateful that my doctor is looking out for what's best for me.

August 13th

Today is the anniversary of Dave's passing. I'm grateful, and it did my heart good to read what Kathleen posted on Facebook. Dave would have been grateful, too:

"My dad never met a dog he didn't like. Four years ago today he passed away. Today in his honor I donated to a few Central Florida animal rescues: Pet Alliance of Greater Orlando, Rescue Me Orlando–Shelter Dogs, Inc., Rescuing Animals in Need (RAIN) which is where we got Molly, and the Orange County Humane Society which is where we got Seamus.

I think my dad would have appreciated it."

August 14th

I'm grateful for all the beautiful cards, texts, email, Facebook messages, and calls from my family and friends remembering Dave.

I think this one from Dave's friend, Arnold, sums up how so many of us feel–"We're less because he's gone, but more because of him."

August 15th

For the last few days I keep replaying a video tribute to Dave. It was played at his Wake, and again the following day at his funeral Mass. I love watching it, although viewing it is usually accompanied by my tears.

I'm so grateful that our friend, Joe, created this touching tribute to his friend, Dave.

August 16th

How grateful I am to have memories of incredible vacations that we took with John and his family on his sailboat, the Southern Cross. Each one of those vacations in Canadian waters on our way up the Inside Passage to Alaska was a once in a lifetime adventure.

Wherever we sailed we never knew what great sight or experience was around the bend. We saw bald eagles gliding above us, whales swimming near our boat, shooting stars at night, and islands to explore where we were the only ones on them. The camaraderie of our two families on each of these vacations is something that I'll gratefully always remember.

Tonight as I write in my gratitude journal these sailing memories make me wonder once again what's around the bend.

August 17th

One of the first friends that I made when we moved from New Jersey to Florida was Amy. We were only in the 6th grade. She always was and always will be one of my BFFs.

I was worried when I woke up this morning because I knew that she was going to have a heart catheterization.

This evening I am relieved, happy, and grateful that everything turned out fine. She's my sister by another mother and father.

August 18th

Each evening my friend, Bunny, posts on Facebook that she is about to say a rosary, and she asks if anyone has any special intentions that they would like prayers said. I always have special intentions.

I'm grateful for Bunny and for her kind offer.

August 19th

Yesterday was the anniversary of Dave's funeral. On today's date I always remember something that happened that gave me goosebumps.

Years before Dave ever got sick, he and I had a conversation about getting a "message" from someone we loved, shortly after they passed away. For Dave, it was his grandmother. For me, it was my Aunt Delia.

Not being a person who liked to talk about death, I made light of our conversation and told him that if he "croaked" before I did, I expected a message from him. He laughed and said that he'd try.

I was happy that the night of the funeral there were many friends and family in our house. At some point during the evening I went into our bedroom and had a one-sided conversation with Dave. It was pretty emotional, and I told him that he couldn't just leave me so suddenly. I told him that I still needed him, and I always would. I asked him to please give me a sign that he was with me.

The following evening when I was in the grocery store I got goosebumps when I looked at the weekly ad that had started the day of the funeral. That's when I saw the sign I had asked from Dave.

Part of the ad was devoted to the pharmacy. There was a picture of a pill bottle. The name on the bottle said David Brown. I know that it didn't have an "e" at the end of the Browne, but it was close enough. The medication on the pill bottle was the only medication that Dave was prescribed. Also, there was an odd note on the bottle that said "Tennessee prescriber." Dave was from Tennessee.

The best part of all was the address that was listed on the top right of the bottle–1 Love.

A coincidence? I don't think so.

Today I'm grateful for this message from Dave.

August 20th

It didn't rain this evening when I took Molly for a walk. It was the first time in a week.

Molly and I are both grateful.

August 21st

I'm grateful today for Alvin at my credit card company. I've been with this company for a long time, and until today I've never had a problem activating the new card which will be replacing a soon to be expired old card.

I was concerned about this issue because important automatic payments are made each month through this card.

Alvin helped me accomplish what needed to be done to activate the new card, and to get this worry off my plate.

August 22nd

When I went to the grocery store today I saw that the fresh frozen flounder fillets that I always buy for $10.99 for a package of three fillets had a sign that said they were on sale for $3.99 a package. I thought that the sale had ended a few days earlier, but because of the sign I figured that the sale had been extended. I took two packages.

When I was checking out they rang up at $10.99 each. I told the cashier about the sale sign, and she sent the bag boy to confirm what I had said.

I'm grateful that I got the two packages for $3.99 each, and that I had yummy flounder for supper.

August 23rd

When I was walking Molly this evening I gasped at one point because I thought that I was about to see a large turtle get run over by a car. This is what happened:

As we approached a sharp curve in the road I saw the turtle crossing the narrow street as a car was about to enter the curve. I didn't know if the driver saw the turtle, but thankfully both he and the passenger saw it and quickly stopped their car. Two teenagers got out of the car and watched as the turtle continued to slowly tiptoe across the street. Each of them told the other to pick up the turtle so that it wouldn't get squashed by a car that was coming from the other direction.

I heard one of them ask the other, "Do you think it's a snapping turtle?"

The answer was "I don't know, but you need to get it out of the road before that car gets here."

I closed my eyes. When I opened them, one of the boys was carrying the turtle into a yard that leads to the lake.

When he returned to his car I thanked him for his kindness, and I told him that I was sincerely grateful that he saved the turtle.

August 24th

I'm getting a bit nervous about my appointment in two days with the dermatologist.

I'm grateful that Kathleen texted me to say that if my leg hurts after the procedure on Wednesday that she'll come over after work to walk Molly. She texted again later in the evening with more words of encouragement, and to say that my leg will be fine.

August 25th

I'm extremely sentimental and will seldom get rid of something just because it's old. Today when I grabbed a decades-old baby food grinder from my pantry, I reminisced about the day that my mom, Michael, and I were at the mall, and my mom spotted it on a shelf. Michael was still eating baby food, and my mother asked if I wanted to make his food for him, rather than always buying it.

Even though that idea had never occurred to me, I said, "Sure." Mom took the grinder off the shelf, paid for it, and gave it to me.

The days of making baby food for Michael, and later Kathleen, are long gone, but I've used that little grinder countless times since they had a need for it. Today I used it to chop up an onion for a meatloaf that I was making. When I was done using it, I carefully washed it, put it gingerly back into the pantry, and thought about that moment in time with my mom, my baby, and the gift she bought me.

I'm sincerely grateful that the grinder still works, and I'm grateful that I still have this sweet memory.

August 26th

I'm thankful that this long awaited day is behind me. The dermatologist froze the precancerous area on my leg. As much as I like the doctor and his staff, I'm grateful that I don't need to return to his office until December.

August 27th

I haven't felt comfortable going inside my church since the pandemic began. Even though the Diocese reopened the churches in May, and there are safety precautions in place, I'm just not ready yet. Today, however, I thought of something that happened inside my church last year that I'm grateful for, although it's mixed with a bit of embarrassment.

It happened shortly before Easter which was the incentive for a lot of people to receive the Sacrament of Reconciliation. Priests from other parishes were helping out and were situated throughout the church. Since I don't like sitting face to face with a priest to confess my sins, I waited in a long line in the side chapel to have the privacy of a confessional.

The line was moving at a snail's pace and I was really hungry. When my stomach started growling loud enough for those around me to hear, I bit the bullet and went into the main church where the lines waiting for a priest were all short.

I waited for just a few minutes for a priest who looked pleasant. We each sat in a chair facing each other and I began by saying, "Bless us, O Lord, and these, Thy gifts, which we are about to receive from Thy bounty, through Christ, our Lord, Amen."

The priest responded, "Let's start over. Bless me, Father, for I have sinned..."

I guess I was hungrier than I thought because I initially said the prayer that Catholics say before eating a meal.

Looking back to last year, I'm grateful for having been able to receive the Sacrament of Reconciliation, for absolution, and for the priest who was as kind as he looked.

August 28th

Once again, I'm grateful for cream sherry. Well, not actually for the cream sherry itself, but for the employee in the grocery store who opened the bottle for me.

It's a twist off top, and I'm never able to get it open. When Dave was alive it was a non-issue, but now it has become one.

Each time I purchase a bottle I ask an employee if they'll open it for me. Sometimes, I get a strange look. Once I was told "No."

I'm grateful for days like today when the person just smiles and says, "Okay."

August 29th

I'm grateful for the majestic sunrise that started my day. Happy endorphins for me!

August 30th

This may seem like a small thing, but not to me.

My computer's mouse stopped working. I didn't know if that meant that I needed to buy a new mouse, or if it would be an easy fix. I brought my laptop, along with its mouse, to the closest computer store.

I'm thankful that the experts don't laugh or roll their eyes when I ask them the most basic questions. Today I'm grateful to Victor who quickly figured out the problem, and fixed it. My mouse just needed new batteries.

Pandemic life would be so much less stressful if all problems were this easy to resolve.

August 31st

I finally got a little yardwork done today that I've been putting off. It helped tremendously that I had some company.

A beautiful large hawk perched on my fence, watching me as I watched him. Perhaps I got closer to him than I should have, but I never felt threatened. I don't think that he did either. I talked to him for a minute or two, but he just stared at me.

I'm grateful that on this hot and humid August day, being one with nature for a few minutes was the encouragement I needed to get the trimming done, and to soothe my soul.

SEPTEMBER

September 1st

I used to donate blood on a regular basis most of my adult life. I enjoyed giving the gift of life to others. Since I've had breast cancer I haven't donated, and I sincerely miss doing it.

I was grateful to hear that Kathleen donated her blood today. I'm proud of her.

September 2nd

Today I remembered that last year at this time while Hurricane Dorian slowly made its way across Florida, CCTN (Catholic Community Television Network) broadcast their interview with me about my first book.

I was humbled that CCTN asked me for an interview, and I'm grateful that the interview gave my story more exposure.

September 3rd

There was a beautiful rocket launch today from the Kennedy Space Center that I could see from my back yard. Even though the Space Center is an hour away, the bright light from the solid rocket boosters made it look like it was much closer.

I've been watching these launches since I was a kid, and they never get old. I'm grateful to have this awesome opportunity.

September 4th

I picked up Molly's prescription dog food from her vet today. Their office is about 45 minutes from my house, and I brought her with me because she loves car rides. I had already paid for the dog food before I left my home, and when I pulled into their parking lot I called them to say that we had arrived.

I'm grateful that Jenn carried the big bag to my car, and I'm grateful for her response to a question that I had. I asked her if I needed to make an appointment to have Molly weighed. She told me that since I was already there that she could weigh her today.

Due to the pandemic, I still couldn't go inside the building. I was grateful that Jenn brought Molly inside and weighed her. Jenn's kindness saved me another 90-minute round trip drive just to get her weighed.

September 5th

I'm grateful for something I saw on this evening's walk. It was a pretty wooden box filled with books for the purpose of a neighborhood book exchange. It was situated right by the sidewalk, and the sign said that you can take a book, donate a book, or do both.

I thought it was a great and "novel" idea!

September 6th

Kathleen, Molly, and I went to a nearby Farmer's Market today. I think that Molly enjoyed the outing as much as we did. I felt safe from COVID- 19 because the booths were all outside, everyone was wearing a mask, and was staying socially distanced.

The booths circled around a pretty lake. It's the same lake that my parents and I used to fish in when I was a little girl. As I walked from booth to booth with my daughter and my dog I was remembering my mom, my dad, and me having fun times around that same little lake.

Tonight as I write in my journal I'm grateful for the time I got to spend with my daughter today, and for memories of happy times from long ago.

September 7th

I'm grateful for a string of texts that I received from Kathy, a friend and classmate from high school. In one of her texts she told me that she thinks of me every day.

I have to admit that during the pandemic there have been days when I've felt isolated from my friends and family. It's a feeling that I've never experienced before in my life.

When I read Kathy's unexpected words today, my heart filled with gratitude.

September 8th

I'm grateful for the eight week Discovering Christ course that started tonight through my church. We will participate through a

Zoom meeting each Tuesday evening since COVID-19 has prevented us from meeting in person.

I appreciate that Mary-Jeanine spent a lot of time with me before the session began trying to help me with my microphone. Even though we weren't successful in getting it to work, I'm thankful for her efforts.

It was great to see and hear the other participants, and I'm really looking forward to being a part of this group for the next seven weeks.

September 9th

I'm grateful for my friend, Annie, and for the jars of homemade muscadine jam and pears that she sent to me all the way from Louisiana. I had never tasted muscadine jam before today, and it sure was delicious on my toast.

I have a feeling that a pear cobbler is in my future.

September 10th

We've had a lot of rain recently, and it appeared that I had a leak in my new roof which damaged a portion of the ceiling in my bathroom. To say that I wasn't happy is an understatement considering the roof is barely a year old. I called the roofing company yesterday, and today a project manager came to my house.

Louis assessed the problem and determined that the vent pipe cover on the roof in the area over the leak had not been properly sealed when the new roof was installed.

I'm grateful that Louis quickly found the problem. I'm also grateful that he not only resealed the vent pipe cover that had the problem, but he proactively resealed all the vent pipe covers on the roof so that there won't be any future problems.

September 11th

My doctors have recommended that I take a few over-the-counter vitamins and supplements. One of the supplements is krill. It's a bit pricey, but if it's good for me I'll buy it.

Today it was on sale as a BOGO which doesn't happen too often. I'm grateful that today I saved over $43.00 on a bottle of krill.

September 12th

On my morning walk I noticed something that never caught my attention before today. I wasn't too far from my house when I heard a bird singing high in a tree. When I looked up I saw a big bright moon in a cloudless blue sky. The moon was framed by green tree branches in the shape of a heart.

I'm grateful for the little bird's singing and for this beautiful sight to behold.

September 13th

I was pleasantly surprised today when Kathleen stopped by for a visit. She brought pastries for me and for her, and a toy for Molly.

I'm always grateful when I get to spend time with her and to know that she wants to spend time with me.

September 14th

I've always appreciated that my friends and family are so encouraging to me, but I've been particularly grateful during the pandemic. During this difficult time several long-time acquaintances have become friends, as we've gotten to know each other better through social media. And family and long-term friends have stayed close, as we reach out to each other more often.

In the last several days I think I've been at the receiving end of a ton of support, as kind calls and texts have increased. One friend said that I was an inspiration; another called me an angel. Messages like those have brightened my days in a way that I hope that I brighten theirs.

I'm grateful that we're here for each other.

September 15th

Kathleen and Facebook both reminded me that my first book, *I'll Love Ye Forever: A Mother and Daughter's Journey Through Long Term Care,* turned two years old today.

Even though things involving the book have pretty much come to a standstill due to the pandemic, I'm grateful for the fun ride it had been pre-pandemic. I look forward to a day when that ride will start up again.

September 16th

I had a routine doctor's appointment today with my oncologist. I'm grateful for how easy the appointment went.

Ever since I had breast cancer it's been difficult to draw my blood. It often takes two different lab techs to be able to get my blood. Today Kaylee got what she needed right away, and I felt no pain.

While I waited for the doctor in the exam room, Rochelle, the doctor's physician assistant, spent a lot of time with me patiently answering my questions.

After the doctor did the exam, she said that everything looked great. She was able to give me the results of some of the blood work that was just performed, and she said everything looked normal. The results of the rest of the tests will take a few more days to know.

She also told me that the pill that I've been taking for the last 10 years to prevent my cancer from returning will be stopped at the end of February. She said that I've been on it long enough.

I'm so grateful for a good checkup and to know that I'll soon be off the pill that has caused serious side effects.

September 17th

Tomorrow is my birthday. I'm grateful for my mom who gave me a birthday.

My mother was in her 40s when she and my dad got married. She told me that she was thrilled when she found out that she was expecting a baby. There were complications, however, that caused a difficult pregnancy.

She found out that she had huge uterine tumors which the doctors said left little room inside her for a baby to grow. Her doctors told her that due to her advanced age she risked her baby being born with Down syndrome. Her doctors also told her that she risked dying if she tried to carry a baby to full term. The doctors suggested that they take the baby. That was an old fashioned euphemism for abortion.

My mom told her doctors that she wouldn't do anything to harm her baby, and if her baby was going to die that she wanted to go with him or her.

Throughout my life my mother often said, "God knew what He was doing when He gave ye to me."

I love you, and I miss you, Mom. Thank you.

September 18th

I'm grateful for the wonderful birthday I had today.

All week Michael, Kathleen, and Aaliya asked me how I wanted to celebrate my birthday. I told them sincerely that all I wanted was to get to spend time with them. They asked me if I wanted to eat at a restaurant or if they could bring food to my house. I haven't eaten in a restaurant since March and really liked the idea of eating in one. I was a bit hesitant, however, because of COVID- 19, so I called my oncologist and internist. They each told me to have a good time, but to wear a mask, social distance, and to use hand sanitizer.

We had a great dinner at a restaurant that I've wanted to go to for years. The food was delicious, but being surrounded by my kids was the best part of the evening. When it was time for desert we decided to go to a nearby ice cream shop.

We had taken two cars for the evening. Michael and Aaliya were in one of them. Kathleen and I were in the other. When we were leaving the first restaurant Michael's car wouldn't start. That had never happened before. He tried jump starting the battery, but had no luck. The restaurant's manager tried helping, but still no luck.

Michael decided to leave his car in the parking lot and to call a tow truck the first thing in the morning to have it towed to the shop that he's used in the past. However, he needed his car by Tuesday morning and asked if he could borrow mine if his wasn't fixed by then. Of course, I said, "Sure."

Kathleen drove the four of us to the ice cream shop where we had yummy ice cream and more great conversation. She later drove us all back to our respective homes. When she got back to her apartment, she texted us to say that 11 police cars had driven quickly past her with their blue lights flashing.

I had a gut feeling that something really bad had occurred, and I was grateful that we all made it safely home.

September 19th

This morning Aaliya drove back to the restaurant to meet the tow truck driver. When she arrived at the restaurant's parking lot she unlocked Michael's car and tried to start it one last time.

It started immediately. She turned it off and tried it again. It started right away. Even though it appeared that everything was okay, she still had it towed to the shop for them to figure out what caused the problem last night that kept it from starting.

Throughout the day I thought about Kathleen's text from last night and the 11 police cars with their flashing blue lights. Michael, Aaliya, and Kathleen don't live far from where the speeding police cars were driving. Perhaps if Michael's car didn't have a problem last night, his or Kathleen's car may have been involved in an accident that would have changed our lives forever.

I'm sincerely glad that his car didn't start last night. I'm grateful for Divine Intervention.

September 20th

I've been putting off having my car serviced due to COVID-19 concerns. However, I felt that I needed to have the routine maintenance done today since Michael might need my car for a long drive on Tuesday.

I'm grateful that the dealership's waiting areas really weren't that crowded. I'm also grateful for the awesome service writer—Fabian. Even though my car is 14 years old, he told me that it was in good condition, and he didn't try to sell me additional services.

September 21st

The auto repair shop called Michael to say that throughout the day today they started his car a dozen times. Each time, the car started immediately and diagnostics could not find any problems. I'm grateful that he won't be facing an expensive car repair.

Based on that phone call, Michael told me that he wouldn't need to borrow my car tomorrow.

I told him that I had an uneasy feeling about him driving his quirky car to an important destination an hour away. It's crucial that he makes it there, and that he arrives on time. I asked him to please drive my car.

He told me that sometimes there's "something" to my feelings. I'm grateful that he acquiesced to my request and will be driving my car tomorrow.

September 22nd

Michael returned my car to me this afternoon, and after a short visit he left with his car.

Kathleen's apartment lease was up today. She rented a truck to move the last of her furniture out of her apartment and into her new abode. She did that with Michael's help.

Later in the evening she texted me to say that Michael had a flat tire on his car, but there were no punctures in the tire.

I'm so grateful that he took my car today instead of his, and I'm grateful for more Divine Intervention.

September 23rd

I'm grateful to Galen. He works for my lawn service company, and today he went above and beyond to help me. There was a big fat frog, or maybe it was a toad, standing his ground by my hose spigot. It was the biggest frog/toad I've ever seen, and he appeared to have no intention of moving.

I asked Galen if he would do me a huge favor and move it. He said that he'd move it to a far corner of my yard.

After he moved it, I thanked him and told him that particular frog/toad gave me the willies. Galen told me that it gave him the willies, too.

September 24th

I called Louis from the roofing company to ask if he would go to my rental property and check all the vent pipe covers and the skylight to make sure that they are all properly sealed. I told him that I was concerned that perhaps the same crew was used to install the roof on the rental that was used to install the roof on my house that had a leak.

I told him that I was going to have to pay to fix the damage in my bathroom that the leak created, and I didn't want to risk having to do the same thing at the rental.

I'm grateful that Louis said that he would be happy to check on the rental property's roof, and that he would reseal the skylight or any vent pipe covers that needed to be resealed. He said that it may take a few weeks before he could fit it into his schedule. I told him that was fine with me.

I was pleasantly surprised when he told me that I won't need to pay to have the damage in my bathroom repaired. He said that the roof's warranty will totally cover those expenses.

Wow! I'm grateful to hear that news!

September 25th

I am grateful that the hair salons are still open, and that Cristina was able to safely cut my hair today. It wasn't until the salons were all closed that I fully realized how much I appreciated them being open.

September 26th

I'm grateful that my good friend, Barb, will be visiting from out of town this weekend. Even though she refuses to sleep at my house because she doesn't want to risk any possibility of giving me COVID-19, we'll be spending time together while socially distancing.

I haven't seen her in months, and I'm so looking forward to this weekend's visit.

September 27th

Today is my mom's birthday. I miss her every day but particularly on special days like today.

If I could have picked from all the women in the world the one

I wanted to be my mother, my mom is the one I would have chosen. I have so many reasons to be grateful for her, but I'll only mention one of them today.

I will always be grateful that many years ago when she was a 17-year-old girl in Ireland, she made the decision to leave her family and her home, get on the ship all by herself, and immigrate to America.

I don't think I'll ever be as brave as my mother was, but I'm full of gratitude that she was.

September 28th

I'm grateful for all that my neighbor, Cathy, does for me, but during my birthday month she has really gone out of her way to celebrate my birthday.

She brought me roses and tomatoes from her gardens; she treated me to takeout from a Tex-Mex restaurant; and she brought me delicious homemade brownies.

Not only is Cathy a blessing to me, she's a blessing to all her neighbors. Three times a week, after the garbage truck has emptied the garbage cans and recyclable bins, Cathy brings the cans and bins from the street back to where they belong outside her neighbors' houses.

She's a wonderful neighbor, and I'm grateful that she's mine.

September 29th

I'm grateful that today is National Coffee Day.

I went to a nearby donut shop and bought a chocolate covered donut with sprinkles to go along with my free coffee. I haven't indulged in a donut in years, but I thought that it would be a great treat in the middle of a pandemic.

Yes, it was.

September 30th

I remember years ago Dave and I wondered if the cost of gas would ever go below $3.00 a gallon again. At that time, it was well over $4.00 a gallon.

I'm grateful that today the price of gas has once again dipped under $2.00 a gallon.

OCTOBER

October 1st

Today was one of those days that I spent time daydreaming about Dave.

In my mind's eye I pictured an evening when we were still dating, and he was walking me up the stairs to my apartment. I don't remember what I said or did that caused him to smile at me and say, "Life with you would be an adventure." That was long before he proposed, but those words made me think that someday he would be more than just a boyfriend.

He was right, and for decades we shared a life together filled with lots of adventures. One of those adventures that I thought about today was one of the trips we took with my mom to Ireland. Like most of our vacations in Ireland with my mom, she'd stay with her brother, or sisters, or nieces, or nephews for a part of the trip while Dave and I would go off by ourselves for a week or so and explore the island.

This particular vacation I thought that it would be fun and exciting to go to Northern Ireland. I'm not sure how I convinced Dave to go along with my plans, but he did, even though he wasn't keen on the idea. This was during the 1980s which was the peak of "The Troubles" in Northern Ireland. It was a time of hunger strikes, and car bombings, and house burnings, and the source of news stories throughout the world.

Shortly after we crossed the border, we had only driven a few miles when we were flagged down and pulled over to the side of the road. Dave rolled down his window and was told to take off his sunglasses. Then the conversation went something like this:

"Didn't I tell you last week when you were here that we didn't want you here?"

"We've just crossed the border a few minutes ago for the first time. We've never been in Northern Ireland before," Dave said.

"You look just like a fella that we talked to last week. What's your purpose here?"

"Sir, my wife and I are tourists. We just wanted to spend a few days in the North," Dave answered.

After a few more questions, the officer said, "Okay, you can go ahead and leave now, but be sure to mind the speed limits through the villages or we'll give you a ticket."

"I'll mind the speed limits," Dave said, and then he continued driving.

When it came time for lunch we drove through a few towns looking for a place to eat. We were surprised to learn that we couldn't park the car in the town unless one of us stayed in the car. If we were both going to leave the car, we had to park it a good distance away from the city center. That was because there had been so many car bombs.

The nights that we were in Northern Ireland we stayed in Bed and Breakfasts. Throughout those nights we could hear guns being fired.

During the day we did a lot of things that both Dave and I enjoyed. We went on scenic drives, walked in a pretty forest, we watched tweed being made, and we took a tour of the Belleek Pottery Factory. We also brought home a memory that neither of us ever forgot.

That happened on a day that we had gotten a little lost. Dave wasn't one to ask for directions. I always asked for directions which is what we did on this particular afternoon.

We pulled up to a building with a young soldier standing in front of it. The Uzi on his hip didn't look very friendly, however. We remained in our car and we were having a good conversation with this soldier when a much older soldier came up to us from the side of the building. He asked if he could help us.

I told him "No" and said that we were about to leave but that I wanted to take a picture first. My camera was on my lap. I was told that if I took a picture of any of the soldiers that they would have to confiscate my camera. He then told us to enjoy our time in Northern Ireland, and he walked back from where he came. All I can say about what happened next is ... the devil made me do it.

Today I'm grateful that this memory came back to me, and how blessed I am for the fun life I shared with Dave.

October 2nd

I've recently been driving my car with a small crack in the windshield. I knew that even though it's quite small that it needed to be repaired.

Today I called my car insurance company and I'm grateful for all the help that I received from Sheila. She walked me through the process, told me that I wouldn't have to pay anything to get it fixed, and that filing this claim wouldn't raise my car insurance premium. She coordinated everything with the glass repair company and told me that someone would come to my house to repair my windshield early next week.

October 3rd

The second reading at this evening's Mass was Paul to the Philippians 4:6-9. I'm grateful for this reading. I really needed to hear these words today.

Verse 6 says, "Do not be anxious about anything, but in everything by prayer and supplication with thanksgiving, let your request be known to God. And the peace of God which surpasses all understanding will guard your hearts and your minds in Christ Jesus."

October 4th

Today is the feast day of St. Francis of Assisi, the patron saint of animals. Each year on this feast day there is a blessing of pets at my church. Dogs, cats, birds, hamsters, rabbits, and any other pet a parishioner may have are brought by their owners to a designated area on parish grounds where they are individually blessed by a priest or a deacon.

Last year when it was Molly's turn, she bowed her head, squatted, and then made a big poop as the deacon was saying a blessing over her. Needless to say, I was a bit embarrassed.

Due to the pandemic, this year's pet blessing was cancelled, but thanks to my friend, Gail, Molly still received a blessing. Gail works for the parish, and she brought two pet blessing kits over to my house. Each kit was made up of the blessing prayer, and a small bottle of holy water. One was for Molly, and the other was for Kathleen's cat, Tiger. At 20 years old, Tiger needs all the blessings he can get.

I'm grateful that Gail thought of Kathleen and me, and our fur babies, and I'm grateful for her kindness in bringing me the pet blessing kits.

October 5th

I've had a little cough for a few days which made me wonder if it was okay to get my flu shot. I called my doctor's office to confirm that I wouldn't have a problem.

The receptionist set up a telehealth appointment for me with their physician assistant. Later in the day she called me and answered all my questions via Facetime.

I was grateful that the PA could allay my concerns without having to go into the doctor's office. I'll be getting a flu shot at the end of the week.

October 6th

I'm grateful that my windshield's crack was repaired today, and that the entire process was simple.

I received a text and an email yesterday saying that Wilfredo would be at my house between 8 a.m. and noon. They sent a picture of Wilfredo so that I would know whom to expect.

Today he arrived at the appointed time. When he got out of his truck he put on a face mask, repaired the crack on my windshield in less than 45 minutes, and then, as Dave used to say, "Bob's your uncle."

October 7th

Since COVID-19 was declared a pandemic way back in March, I haven't had much to look forward to. These days, going to the grocery store is an adventure.

This evening I am grateful for a question that Michael asked me–"Mom, would you like to go on a family vacation next year with us?"

Happy tears to have something like that to look forward to, and heartfelt gratitude that my son would want me to come along.

I am blessed.

October 8th

Health insurance, car insurance, and homeowner's insurance aren't important until we need to use them.

Today I'm grateful for Barbara, the agent for my homeowner's insurance for one of the rentals. That policy recently renewed, but I didn't take the time to read it over carefully before its renewal because it's one that we've had for a long time. I didn't think that there were any issues. I should have read it.

The policy includes a charge which has a $20,000.00 deductible. It also includes a similar sounding charge with a $500.00 deductible.

Barbara took the time to speak with the underwriters' department to confirm that those two charges pertain to the same natural disaster– sinkholes. She was told that both include sinkhole coverage, but the one with the higher deductible would cover more of the damage. They also told her that if I wanted to make any changes to my policy that I needed to have done it prior to the policy having been renewed.

I'm grateful for Barbara's help today, and that she's already put my issue on her calendar prior to the policy's next renewal. We'll discuss these charges in more detail at that time.

Without Dave I don't know what I don't know, but I'm learning.

October 9th

I'm grateful that I was able to receive my annual flu shot today.

I've been getting one each year since my oncologist told me when I was diagnosed with breast cancer that he would not start my chemo until Dave, Michael, Kathleen, and I received the flu shot.

I'm grateful for the vaccination, and that I haven't had the flu or any side effects from the vaccine throughout the years. I'll be equally grateful when there is a safe vaccine for COVID- 19.

October 10th

It's often hard to do or say the hard things. I'm grateful that today I was able to do both.

October 11th

Yesterday evening I was walking Molly through my front yard towards the street to start our walk. While we were still on the grass she yelped, then jumped, and then tucked her tail between her legs. She held her paw up, and she immediately started limping.

I looked at her paw and didn't see anything out of the ordinary. I felt her paw pads and between her toes, but still no evidence of what hurt her. I have a feeling that it was a wasp. Since she clearly wasn't able to go for a walk, I brought her back into the house.

She continued to walk with a limp all evening, and she wasn't able to get herself up on the couch. I was worried and called the emergency pet clinic. I told them what had happened and asked if I should bring her to their clinic.

They said that they didn't think that it was necessary and told me what to watch out for during the night. If certain things were to happen, they said to bring her to the emergency clinic. They also said that if she wasn't better by the morning, I needed to bring her to her vet.

She's my morning alarm. She comes into my bedroom each morning around the same time and makes her happy Molly sounds. This morning I was worried when this daily routine didn't happen.

I quickly got out of bed and searched for her. I found her in her crate. That's her safe place, and that's where she goes when she's afraid or when I'm not at home. As soon as she saw me she got out of her crate with her tail wagging, and she smiled at me. She was no longer limping.

Even though she seemed back to normal, I made an appointment with her doctor. I wanted to make sure that the vet didn't detect any issues that I wasn't seeing.

I am so very grateful that the vet didn't see anything to be concerned about, and that Molly appears to be totally recovered. I'm happy that she was eager to go for a walk this evening.

October 12th

I'm grateful for a "How've you been?" text that I received today from my friend, Stephanie. We became friends many years ago when we both worked at the State Attorney's Office. We were close enough friends that I asked her to be one of my bridesmaids.

Even though we don't see or speak with each other too often anymore, we have that wonderful type of friendship that when we do get together it's like we spoke only yesterday.

October 13th

Barry, my cousin Paula's husband, passed away a few days ago. I'm deeply saddened by his passing, but I'm grateful that I was able to watch the funeral through Zoom. I'm also grateful that Kathleen was able to watch it with me.

Last summer Kathleen and I flew to Atlanta to celebrate Barry's birthday. I am so grateful that we did.

Carpe Diem.

October 14th

A year ago today I had my annual appointment with my surgical oncologist. This was an appointment that Dave used to go to with me each year. Since he's passed away, Ninetta, one of my BFFs since we were kids, goes along with me.

Last year on this date, early in the morning she drove from her house on the east coast of Florida to my house in Central Florida. From my house, she drove me to my appointment on the west coast of the state.

At the end of my appointment last year, my doctor told me that everything looked fine, and that he wanted me to make my next appointment for 10/12/2020. Due to COVID-19, I have yet to schedule a new appointment.

I've recently spoken with Ninetta about this appointment that I need to schedule, and I asked her whether she would be able to go with me.

Without any hesitation my forever friend answered, "Sure."

I'll always be grateful for Ninetta.

October 15th

I know that between work and school that Michael has very little spare time these days. I was happy to see him this morning when he stopped by for a visit on his way to work at the hospital. I fixed him breakfast and we had time for some mom/son talk.

I am happy, grateful, and blessed to have gotten this visit from my son.

October 16th

I drove to the Tax Collector's Office today to pay for a new registration sticker for my car because the old one was about to expire. During pre-pandemic days this visit always involved a long wait.

When I reached the front entrance, I read the sign on the door that said that appointments were now necessary. Since I didn't have one, I went inside to see if I could make one with their help or if I had to do it myself online.

I'm grateful that the clerk told me that between the hours of 8 a.m. and 2 p.m. an appointment wasn't necessary. Since it was only 10 a.m. she asked how she could help me. I told her that I just needed to renew my car's registration. She gave me a number and said that the wait shouldn't be long.

She was correct. Less than 10 minutes after I arrived, I was leaving with a new sticker for my car.

Today I'm grateful for the quickest visit I ever had at the Tax Collector's Office.

October 17th

I received a text tonight from my neighbor, Flo. She said that her husband, George, was going through my yard to walk a turtle to the lake. She wanted to let me know because it was dark outside, and she didn't want me to be concerned if I saw a man in my yard at night.

I'm grateful for her thoughtful text because I probably would have felt uneasy if Molly started barking, and I saw the shadow of a man walking at night in my yard.

I'm also grateful for George's kindness in getting the turtle back to where it belonged so that it wouldn't get run over by a car on our dark street.

October 18th

Last night I thought that I had COVID- 19. I had a sore throat, was achy, felt worn out, and I had a low grade fever. I tried my best not to think about a COVID- 19 diagnosis, and took an Ibuprofen in hopes of feeling better.

I don't know what was going on with me last night, but this morning I woke up feeling just fine.

I'm grateful that I don't have COVID- 19.

October 19th

I texted our friend, Joe, today to thank him for creating the beautiful website for my first book. The website is called The Sandwiched Boomer and it can be found at sandwichedboomer.com

Even though he designed it two years ago, I'm still so grateful how it turned out, and for the compliments that it still receives. I'm also grateful that Joe texted me back to say to let him know if I need any updates made to the website.

I've been blessed with wonderful friends.

October 20th

I voted today, along with a lot of other people who were all wearing face masks and who seemed to be in a good mood. I'm grateful that I live in a country where my voice and my vote matters.

October 21st

I'm grateful for Melissa and Leslie who work in my dentist's office. They have answered the same question for me several times, and they never lose patience or sound annoyed that I keep asking.

I have dental insurance, but the Explanation of Benefits that I receive always shows I have a balance. Sometimes, it's been for hundreds of dollars.

When I speak to Melissa or Leslie they always assure me that I have a -0- balance. Today when I called with that same question, I told Melissa that every time I receive an Explanation of Benefits that shows that I owe money, I will continue to call to confirm that I don't. I told her that I hoped that was okay with her.

She couldn't have been kinder or more accommodating when she said, "No problem."

October 22nd

I'm taking a break from social media which is highly unusual for me. I used to post something on Facebook regularly, and I have to say that I enjoyed the feedback that my posts generated.

I didn't announce that I was taking a break. I just went dark, with the exception of responding to private messages.

I was pleasantly surprised to find out that some of my Facebook friends noticed that I haven't been on Facebook recently. I've received a handful of messages and texts asking if I'm okay. A few of them said that they were worried about me.

I'm grateful for these friends who not only noticed when I suddenly stopped posting, but also checked on me.

October 23rd

Today I am grateful for my friend, Patti, and I'm thankful for a beautiful and uplifting email that she sent me. The email contains a story that's definitely religious, but it's also a story that the reader, no matter what their religion is, would find comforting. I liked it so much that I shared it with some of my family and friends.

Each of them thanked me for sending it to them and said that it made them feel good.

October 24th

Today is a sad day. My cousin, Sally, in Ireland passed away today. She was one of the first cousins I remember playing with when my mom brought me to Ireland as a child.

When I grew up I always looked forward to visiting Sally and her husband, Tom, their five daughters, and their son. Dave, Michael, and Kathleen enjoyed visiting them, too.

Even though I'm sad today, I'll be forever grateful that she was my cousin. I'll always remember her kindness, her big smile, and her hearty laugh.

October 25th

When I turned on my computer this morning the screen was frozen. I tried a few different things, but to no avail. Not that many years ago, the fix to this sort of problem always occurred when I'd say, "Dave, help me, please."

Since I no longer have that luxury, I did the next best thing. I texted his brother, John.

To say that I'm grateful for John is an understatement. I know that I can always count on him whenever I need help.

He told me to reboot the computer. I thought that I had already done that, but I guess I hadn't held the power button down long enough, or waited long enough to restart it. When I tried it again per John's advice, it started right away.

When I thanked him for helping me fix the problem, he responded by saying, "When in doubt, reboot."

October 26th

Every now and then I've joked that there must be a target on the back of my car. That's because I've been involved in three rear-end collisions which have caused issues with my back throughout the years. Physical therapy has always helped tremendously.

Intensive physical therapy also helped me to walk again after I had been kept in a hospital bed for nearly a month when staph infected my blood during my cancer treatment.

Recently, I've been feeling yucky enough that I think I need PT once again. I was concerned, however, that perhaps there was a lifetime cap on the number of times I could receive physical therapy.

I'm grateful that today when I called my insurance company that I've had for decades, Keith was the representative who answered my call. He was very helpful, and after reading over my policy he assured me that there is not a lifetime cap on physical therapy.

I'm relieved and grateful to know that I'll be able to receive physical therapy whenever it may be needed.

October 27th

I used to have perfect blood pressure. About a year after Dave passed away it was no longer perfect. It had become dangerously high and my doctor immediately put me on blood pressure medication. I guess that between my grief and my new found responsibilities, my blood pressure went through the roof. When the doctor prescribed the medication I told him that I thought my high BP was "situational" and that in time I would no longer need meds.

After having been on the medication for about three years, I've been off it now for more than two weeks. I monitor my BP daily, and I'm grateful to say that my blood pressure is back to being perfect.

October 28th

I received good news today from my friend, Annie. She messaged me to say that her book club has chosen my book about long term care to be on their reading list.

I'm grateful for Annie, and for her book club's decision.

October 29th

The water pressure in my house went way down yesterday. I didn't have a clue what caused the problem, but I hoped that it would somehow resolve itself by the time I woke up this morning. Unfortunately, I woke up with the same water pressure problem that I went to bed with.

When I took Molly outside this morning I noticed that one of the well water pressure tanks on the side of the house was making a lot of noise.

I called Floyd, our well guru. Floyd's dad was the expert that my in-laws called when they lived in our house.

Floyd pulled into my driveway a few hours after I called him. He did his magic in silencing the pressure tank, but said the source of the noise wasn't what caused the low water pressure. He did some more checking and asked if I had water running. I told him I definitely did not. He bent over and put his ear up to the tank and said that water was definitely running. He told me to listen like he did. When I listened at the bottom of the tank, I could hear it, too.

He asked me to go back into the house and check all the faucets. He was going to check all the spigots outside.

There was no water running inside the house, but Floyd found a hose that was connected to a spigot that had been left on, and he turned it off. I don't know who turned it on, or when it was done. He then asked me to go back inside the house and turn a faucet on to test the water pressure. I turned on the water at the kitchen sink. Once again, I have great water pressure.

I'm grateful for Floyd's help, and I'm happy that the problem wasn't a major one. I'm also glad to know what to check for if I ever have low water pressure in the future.

October 30th

I was grateful to start the day with gorgeous weather on my morning walk. The sun peeking through the trees, the cool breeze on my face, and the birds singing created a mood that brought me thoughts of Dave. Most of those thoughts focused on how proud he'd be of our kids.

In the midst of my thoughts I had some company. A big, beautiful butterfly fluttered around me, and stayed with me for the length of two or three houses. It made me smile, and for some odd reason it comforted me.

My day sort of ended like it had begun—with thoughts of Dave. When I was putting my supper dishes into the dishwasher I could see the huge full moon through my kitchen window. I stopped doing the dishes and went out on the back porch.

I could almost feel Dave's arm around my waist as I stared at the beautiful moon reflecting on the lake.

I'm full of gratitude for what I got to experience today—the butterfly, the moon, and thoughts of my love.

October 31st

Today is Dave's birthday. This isn't the first birthday since he's passed away, but I have to admit that for me it's been the toughest one. I think that being in the middle of a pandemic doesn't help. But even on pensive days like today, I know that I have so much to be grateful for.

Michael and Aaliya were both working, but Kathleen came over this evening so that I wouldn't be alone. She walked into the house with a bouquet of sunflowers for me. Sunflowers symbolize unwavering faith and unconditional love.

Then she fixed dinner for us which I really appreciated. I didn't tell her, but I would have been sad eating alone this evening.

I'm grateful that every day I have something to be grateful for. Days like today, I'm extra grateful for what I once had, and for what I still have.

NOVEMBER

November 1st

Even though I haven't been inside my church since the pandemic began, today I went to Michael and Aaliya's church, along with Kathleen. It was for a special service that Michael invited me to attend. Most of the time I sat between Michael and Kathleen, but at one point during the service we stood with our arms around each other. There are no words to describe the love that I felt during those minutes.

After the service was over Michael and Aaliya treated us all to lunch at a restaurant. We each had worn a mask during Church and at the restaurant except when we were eating, but for me today I didn't feel like we were in the middle of a pandemic. It felt normal.

I'm so grateful for normalcy and for the wonderful day I got to spend with my kids. No matter how old they are, they'll always be my "kids."

November 2nd

Every year for Halloween I buy lots of candy. This pandemic year was no different. I didn't know if there would be anyone coming to my door, but I didn't want to disappoint any trick-or-treaters who might come.

No one came.

Now that Halloween is behind us for another year, I wasn't sure what I would do with the candy. I asked a few friends if they wanted it, but everyone I asked was in the same situation that I was in.

I thought that since the bags of candy were unopened and I still had the receipt, perhaps I could return them to the store.

I'm grateful to Rita, the sweet cashier who graciously took them back and gave me a full refund.

November 3rd

Thank goodness for Fern, my handyman.

Today he came to my house and replaced a few shutters that had fallen to the ground and broke. I'm sure they had been on the house for 40 years or more. The first one fell while Dave was going through cancer treatment. The second one fell since he passed away.

Replacing those shutters was totally cosmetic and not high on my list of things that needed to be done. I recently changed my mind, however, and decided that I had waited long enough.

I'm grateful that Fern ordered new shutters and installed them today. My house looks like it got a facelift!

November 4th

This evening when I was walking Molly I spotted Mr. Blair in his front yard, and we visited for a few minutes. He's a spry nonagenarian who lives a handful of houses up my street. It's always a pleasure to get to spend time with him. He's the kind of person who makes you feel good just by talking with him.

Long before my kids were in high school, he was the band director at their school. Kathleen was in the band for all four years, and I know she would have loved having him as her band director.

I'm grateful that he lives on my street because he's the only person left who still remembers my in-laws and their Old English Sheepdog, Missy. My father-in-law and Missy wrote a book "together" and they appeared on the old TV show *To Tell the Truth*.

Mr. Blair also remembers when there was a giant alligator that often sunned in our back yard.

I'm sincerely grateful to have Mr. Blair for one of my neighbors, and that I had the opportunity to spend a little time with him this evening.

November 5th

I was entertained to see four large cranes walking on the side of the road heading to the entrance of the mall.

I'm grateful that the cars were giving them a wide berth.

November 6th

John texted me today to tell me to make sure that my phone was up to date with the proper version of the software. He said that there is a serious vulnerability that needs patching. He told me to share this information with Michael, Kathleen, and Aaliya.

I'm always grateful for John, and that today he shared this information with me that I didn't know.

November 7th

I'm not going to say whether I'm glad or sad by the results of the election, but I will say that I'm extremely grateful that today an announcement was finally made.

November 8th

Kathleen stopped by for a surprise visit this evening. While she was here she backed up my phone to the Cloud. This is my first smartphone. I've been using it for more than two years and backing it up to the Cloud wasn't something that I knew I needed to do.

I'm grateful for her help.

November 9th

Those of us who live in Florida have been keeping an eye on Hurricane Eta. It's a huge storm, and I pray that it doesn't come our way. Already, however, we are getting a lot of rain because of it.

I'm grateful to Cathy for checking the radar and for doing a good job at predicting the best time to walk our dogs. Today we squeezed in our walk between two heavy downpours. I was relieved that we only had one light sprinkle along the way.

November 10th

Today is my wedding anniversary. I'm grateful for the decades that I got to spend with my best friend.

Kathleen texted me this morning to say, "Happy Anniversary." She later sent another text that said, "I love you."

I'll never get to hear Dave say those words to me again, or read them in a card, but I'm so grateful that our daughter remembered our special day and texted me the words that her dad would have said.

Most days I have several things that I am grateful for that I write in my personal gratitude journal, but I usually only write one thing that I'm grateful for in my book. Today I'll be writing a second one.

This was another bittersweet day for me because it was an anniversary without Dave. I planned to do my best, however, to make it a happy day. I thought that it might lift my spirits if I quietly celebrated our years together.

I knew that if he was alive we'd be going to a nice restaurant for dinner. This afternoon I decided to go to a nearby family owned Italian restaurant, which was one of our favorites, and order a takeout dinner for tonight. For many years my very favorite item on the menu was lobster ravioli. Most celebrations at that restaurant included lobster ravioli.

When I arrived at the restaurant I went upstairs to the upscale part of the restaurant. There was nobody attending the front desk, but I could hear people talking at the back of the restaurant. I walked to where the people were and saw the cooks conversing with each other. I told one of them that I'd like to order a takeout lobster ravioli. He told me that they weren't open yet.

"Please," I said pitifully.

"We're not open."

"Do you want to know why I want your lobster ravioli?" I asked as the floodgates were about to open.

"Okay," he said as he walked away from where he was preparing food, and stood closer to me.

"Today is my anniversary, and my husband has passed away, and this was one of our favorite restaurants, and I usually ordered lobster ravioli, and if he was alive we'd probably be eating here tonight, and I'd be ordering lobster ravioli. Please can I buy lobster ravioli?"

I was probably hard to understand since I was babbling those words with a mask over my mouth and nose, and my crying had caused my nose to run.

He looked at me and said, "Give me about 10 minutes, and I'll have lobster ravioli ready for you."

I have to emphasize that their lobster ravioli is delicious, but I don't think that my meltdown had anything to do with the ravioli. I think it had everything to do with what it represented in my mind–good times and fun celebrations with Dave.

It probably goes without saying that I'm tremendously grateful to Jake, the cook.

November 11th

I'm still thinking about my anniversary. I will be forever grateful for something that a woman that I barely knew did on my wedding day.

My dad had been in the hospital for nearly three weeks recovering from quintuple heart bypass surgery, which involved all five of the major vessels feeding his heart. I prayed and I prayed that he would be able to walk me down the aisle at my wedding, but that was not to be.

The day before the wedding his doctors told him that he could attend the wedding ceremony, but that he would have to return to the hospital as soon as the Mass was over. He couldn't go to the reception.

His nurses all knew when I was getting married because my dad had told them all. One of those nurses wasn't scheduled to work the day of my wedding and volunteered to take him to it, to stay with him during the ceremony, and then bring him back to his hospital room when the ceremony had ended.

It's because of this kindhearted nurse that my dad was able to see me get married, and to be in a wedding day family picture.

After the reception was over, Dave and I stopped by the hospital to visit my dad before we left on our honeymoon. The nurses that we saw told us that my father told them how proud he was, and that it was the happiest day of his life.

My wedding day would not have been the same if it wasn't for this compassionate woman that I hardly knew. All these years later, gratitude still fills my heart.

November 12th

Yesterday our country celebrated Veterans Day. We owe our veterans a debt of gratitude for all that they have done for each of us. I'm grateful every day for these unsung heroes, four of whom are close to my heart:

Dave served in the Navy during the Vietnam War.

His dad served in the Army during World War II, and was badly injured.

My dad also served in the Army during World War II.

My cousin, Pat, who was like a grandfather to me was born in Ireland, but served in the U.S. Navy during World War I, and World War II where he was injured.

November 13th

I'm grateful that Aaliya invited me to eat dinner tonight at her house with her and Kathleen. It was really nice to have a home cooked meal made by someone other than me.

Even though Michael wasn't able to join us, I thoroughly enjoyed the evening with two of my three kids.

November 14th

Tonight I am grateful for leftovers. The salmon that Aaliya cooked last night was absolutely delicious, and I got to enjoy it again tonight in my home.

November 15th

The water that I use to irrigate my lawn comes from the lake that I live on. Dave installed the entire system. Every now and then when the apparatus in the lake got clogged and the pump wasn't able to pump the water through the pipes, he would put on his waders, go into the lake, and remove whatever was keeping the system from working.

I am grateful to Kevin and Estevan that whenever they mow my lawn, they continue to do what Dave used to do in the lake whenever it's needed. Dave's waders still come in handy.

November 16th

Many years ago I had a boss by the name of Steve. I was the administrator of the large division that he ran. Somewhere along the way he and Dave became close friends, and once a week they would get together after work.

Dave and I were sorry to see an end to our close connection with Steve when he and his family moved far away.

Today I am grateful that all these years later, through an old email address, Steve and I have reconnected. I was happy to hear that his wife and daughters are all doing well, too.

November 17th

As I walked into a store earlier today the sky looked dark and threatening. I tried to make my purchases as quickly as possible so that I wouldn't get drenched walking back to my car, or have to drive home in heavy rain.

I was grateful 20 minutes later when I exited the store that all the clouds had disappeared and the sky was a brilliant blue. The air was so clear that it reminded me of what the view from my car is like after I've cleaned the windshield. I have to say that such a quick change in the weather doesn't happen too often, but I was happy that it happened today.

November 18th

When I was walking Molly I met a lady several blocks from my home who was also walking her dog. We had seen each other many times in the past, but we never stopped to talk. This evening we stopped and had a friendly chitchat.

I'm grateful for a new friend, and for the small talk that we had.

November 19th

Today I am grateful for Corrine. She and I arrived at the entrance to the Post Office about the same time. Actually, she got there right before I did, and she was carrying several boxes. I appreciated her kindness in telling me to get in line ahead of her since I only had one item that needed to be mailed.

In the overall scheme of things, what she did may not be a big deal, but in my mind the little things are important, too.

November 20th

Thanksgiving is nearly a week away, but something happened today that I'm extremely thankful for.

Years ago when Michael and Kathleen were learning to drive, Dave and I would emphasize safety issues that were important to remember. Having lost his mom in a car accident, he really hammered home specific things that a new driver may not always pay attention to. One of those things was obvious but needed repeating—a red light won't stop a car from going through it.

This evening Kathleen told me that she was stopped at a red light earlier today, and she was the first in line. When it turned green she didn't immediately step on the accelerator and go. She told me that at that moment she remembered Dave's advice about waiting and looking both ways before driving. That advice may have saved her life because as she waited an extra moment after her light had turned green, a car ran their red light. They would have T-boned her car if she hadn't waited.

I am grateful, thankful, and blessed that my daughter is safe and sound tonight.

November 21st

I'm grateful for a message that I received today from my cousin, Teresa, in Ireland. Her kind words brought happy tears to my eyes. She told me that she and her family are having a Mass said tomorrow in memory of Dave.

She said that her family often mentions my family in her home. She said that recently her husband, John, and son, Daniel, were reminiscing about the day that they went to a football (soccer) match with Dave and Michael.

It makes me so very happy to know that even though he's gone, his family and friends still reminisce about the times when he was with them. I once heard someone say that we sort of die twice. Once when we're declared dead, and again when people stop remembering us.

I think there is truth in those words.

November 22nd

When I watched the livestreamed Mass today from St. Patrick's Church in Clonbur, Ireland, it made me happy to hear Dave's name mentioned not just once, but two times. I thought that the priest's sermon was awesome, and his words had a lot of meaning for me personally. I think that Dave would have liked the sermon, too.

I'm deeply grateful to my cousin, Teresa, and her family, for thinking of Dave and then requesting this Mass in his memory.

November 23rd

This evening when I was walking Molly, a gentleman came out of his house as we were walking by it. He said that he saw me on TV, and he told his wife that I was the lady who walks Molly each day. I was totally surprised and said, "Really? What was I doing?"

It turns out that he saw the YouTube video of my interview from last year about my long term care book.

Book sales during the pandemic have been down, not because it's not a good book, but because at this time it's difficult to even visit our loved ones in a nursing home. I feel confident that when the pandemic is behind us, my book will once again be a useful read.

I'm grateful and happy to have had this interaction with a neighbor.

November 24th

Today I had another issue to deal with concerning my well water system. This time it had to do with maintenance, not repair.

It's been five years since Dave ordered the carbon filter tank, and every five years the media needs to be replaced. This process is totally Greek to me and at first when I spoke with Al, the representative from the company that Dave bought the tank, I was calling it medium.

I had no idea what the purpose of the media was. Al explained its purpose to me, and he told me what the media consists of. I'm grateful to Al who told me that if I waited three more days to order it that it would probably be on sale for Black Friday. Since I thought that the price of the media was hefty, I took Al's advice and decided to wait a few more days before ordering it.

November 25th

I'm grateful to Louis from the roofing company. Today he went to my rental that had a new roof installed last year. He proactively resealed the skylight and all the vent pipe covers that were on the roof. I think that he did this for me for my peace of mind, and not because it was necessary. He knew that I was worried because of the leak I had in my roof, and that I didn't want the same thing to happen with my rental's roof.

November 26th

Not getting to see Michael, Aaliya, and Kathleen very often during the pandemic hasn't been easy. I am grateful every day for my kids, but I am especially grateful that today, Thanksgiving Day, we gathered together, along with Aaliya's dad, Faz. It was wonderful to get to share a meal and to be thankful together.

Even though we wore masks, ate outdoors, and socially distanced, it was still an awesome day!

Life is good!

November 27th

I bought the media today that I had planned to buy three days ago. I'm grateful to Al for suggesting I wait until today to purchase it. His advice saved me $50.00.

November 28th

I'm grateful that Aaliya sent leftovers home with me from our Thanksgiving dinner. I'll be enjoying food that each of us cooked or baked for a few more days. I'm grateful for comfort food.

November 29th

When Kathleen and I spoke this evening she asked if I'd like to go with her for a weekend over to our condo. It's hard to describe how grateful I am to have a daughter who wants to hang out with her mom.

November 30th

In this month of Thanksgiving I am grateful for my sister, Judy. Our relationship is a loving one, but it is also unusual. That's because I didn't know that I had a sister until I was eight years old. That's when I found out that my dad had been married once before, and that he had a daughter.

I never met Judy until I was in my late 20s. We live on the opposite side of the country from each other. Dave actually met her before I did because of a business trip that he had in the city that she lived in. Since that initial meeting she and her daughter, Cortney, have visited us several times. Dave, Michael, Kathleen, and I have reciprocated.

I can't think of this month of Thanksgiving without thinking of my sister, Judy, and my niece, Cortney. I am grateful and I am blessed.

DECEMBER

December 1st

Today I'm grateful for Katie. She's the mom of my BFF, Amy.

When we were growing up Amy spent lots of time at my house, and I spent lots of time at hers. I fondly remember Katie's delicious Southern cooking, playing board games and card games with her, and the many times that she took us to drive-in movie theaters.

Katie and Amy now live many states away from me. It's been years since I last saw Katie who currently lives in a senior facility, but we still have enjoyable conversations on the phone, even though the news she tells me hasn't always been great during the pandemic.

When we spoke today she told me that her facility is on lockdown, and that Amy can't visit her in her apartment. I could hear the angst in her voice when she let me know that the man across the hall from her has COVID- 19. When we spoke about pleasant things, however, I could hear the smile in her voice, and it did my heart good to once again hear her North Carolina accent.

I'm so blessed that Katie is in my life.

December 2nd

My friend, Lorraine, called me today. She and I used to work together at the State Attorney's Office. I think that she must have had ESP to call me when she did because we were each feeling the social distancing effects of the pandemic.

I'm grateful that Lorraine thought of me and followed up with a call. I think that it was good for both of us.

December 3rd

I'm grateful for Carol who works in scheduling in a local hospital. My oncologist has ordered three tests that she wants me to have done ASAP. It's sometimes difficult to get non-emergency appointments this time of the year because many people who have met their insurance deductible are now scheduling appointments that they've been putting off.

I was happy that Carol was able to get everything scheduled in the next few weeks.

December 4th

I had a chest x-ray today. I'm grateful for two of the ladies who work at the facility where it was done.

After Evelyn signed me in, I explained that there was a mistake on the bill from the last time I was there, and I was having problems getting it resolved. A wrong diagnosis was on the bill that was submitted to my insurance company, and the claim was denied. Even though I've spoken with several people, the problem has yet to be corrected.

Evelyn gave me another phone number and said that was the correct department to help me.

I'm also grateful for Laleh who felt like a friend when she was doing the x-ray.

December 5th

Today is Aaliya's birthday. I am so grateful that she and Michael met, fell in love, and became one. I could not have hoped for a kinder, sweeter, more loving daughter-in-law. I am blessed.

December 6th

I'm grateful that today I had a long talk on the phone with Debra. She's a friend from church and a fellow author. It's been months since we've spoken with each other, and it was great catching up.

We even talked a little bit about book publishing, and I sincerely think that we each may have learned a little something new from the other. That's something to be grateful for, too.

December 7th

I'm so very grateful for one of the best news days I've had in a long, long time.

Michael called me to say that he took his final exam today in nursing school, and he did well. Music to this mother's ears. His dad would be so proud, too.

December 8th

I'm grateful today that the first COVID- 19 vaccine in the world was given. It's a momentous day for all of us on Planet Earth. I pray that this is the beginning of the end of this horrific virus.

December 9th

I had a flashback today of something that happened on a cold December day while I worked at the State Attorney's Office. As a witness coordinator I never knew who I'd be speaking with when I answered the phone. I'm grateful to remember this unlikely conversation that I look back on fondly:

My personal cell phone rings.

"Hello," I said.

"Is this Mrs. Browne?" asked the voice with an Irish brogue.

"It is," I answered.

"This is Helen Carney, private secretary to Mrs. Mary McAleese, President of Ireland," she said.

"Pardon me?"

"Mrs. McAleese asked me to ring you to inquire how your aunt is keeping."

"Delia? She's doing great. Thanks for asking," I answered, totally not believing who was on the other end of the call. THE PRESIDENT OF IRELAND'S OFFICE–OMG!

"We see that she'll be turning 101 next month. We wanted to send her a little something, but we wanted to make sure that she is still with us."

"She's doing well. Thank you for asking, and thank you for your generous gift that the President sent her last year for the Centenarians Abroad. She was flabbergasted when she saw it."

"We enjoy recognizing our Irish emigrants who have been blessed to live to 100. Please let your aunt know that the President sends her regards, and she wishes her a very happy birthday."

After we said our goodbyes, I sat there for a moment thinking how I would answer Dave that evening when he'd ask me if anything interesting happened at work.

That's when my office phone rang.

"Hey, I ain't coming to no court," said a deep angry voice.

"Wanna tell me why not?"...

December 10th

During the pandemic it's sometimes a little difficult to recognize people that we know because of their face mask. Today I thought that I recognized someone that I didn't know.

When I was in the grocery store a tall young lady and I socially distanced as we both looked at the canned soup. She looked familiar and I asked her if she used to play on the Rollins College basketball team with Kathleen. Her eyes smiled and she said, "No," and that she had just recently moved to our area. She told me that her name was Jo. That led to a really nice conversation.

Each morning when I wake up I never know what will happen during my day that I will be grateful for, but I always know there will be something.

Today I'm grateful for that chance encounter with Jo.

December 11th

I'm grateful for the time I got to spend with Michael, Aaliya, and Kathleen trimming the Christmas tree at Michael and Aaliya's house.

That in itself would have been a fun evening, but it didn't stop there. They introduced me to a game called Bananagrams. It was so much fun that I stayed longer than I had intended so that we could play it a second time.

I love learning new things.

December 12th

This evening when I was walking Molly with Cathy and her dog, we saw the most beautiful cloud formations I remember seeing in quite some time. If I had my phone with me I would have taken pictures of them, but I didn't have it.

I'm grateful that Cathy had her phone, took pictures, and later sent them to me.

December 13th

Today I bought gift cards for stocking stuffers from one of my favorite pastry shops. I wanted to also buy a few more at the Tex-Mex restaurant next door, but they weren't open yet, and there wasn't a sign on the door with their hours.

When I was paying for the pastry shop gift cards, I asked Sofia, the cashier, if she knew when the Tex-Mex restaurant would be open. She quickly looked it up for me.

I'm grateful for her kindness, and that she took the time to help me and didn't just say, "I don't have a clue."

December 14th

I'm thankful that the first COVID- 19 shot was given today in the USA. I know that it will be a while before the needle makes it to my arm, but I'm grateful to know that it's going to happen.

December 15th

I'm grateful for something that Kathleen recently did that will put a smile on a lot of children's faces.

She got permission from the property manager of the office building where she works to put out a big box to collect toys for the Baby DJ Christmas Toy Drive. Permission was given, and the number of donations made has been substantial.

During the pandemic she has donated her hair, her blood, her money, and her time to help those in need. I'm a proud mom.

December 16th

Kathleen called this morning to ask if I wanted to meet her at the fruit stand near my house on her lunch break. She wanted to buy some Florida treats for her best friend, Sarah. Sarah, lovingly known by Dave and me as "daughter number two" now lives in California.

I'm grateful for the rendezvous with Kathleen, and that I found some good stocking stuffers to help Santa.

December 17th

As we get closer to Christmas I'm missing Dave all the more.

I'm grateful that as I longed for him today I remembered one of my favorite quotes that's attributed to Dr. Seuss -

"Don't cry because it's over, smile because it happened."

I'm smiling.

December 18th

After COVID- 19 caused my retired friends from the State Attorney's Office and me to stop having our monthly luncheons at restaurants, we decided to try something different today. We met in a pavilion in a beautiful park and had our luncheon there.

It was awesome to see each other, reminisce, and fill each other in on what's been going on since we last got together.

I'm grateful for this great group of friends.

December 19th

I'm grateful for the lady who was sitting on the seat of her walker outside the grocery store. As she sat, she rang the bell for the Salvation Army's donation kettle.

She inspired me.

December 20th

Things are quite a bit different for me during the holidays now that Dave is gone.

Throughout our marriage Dave and I always had a live Christmas tree. Some of them were Charlie Brown looking trees, but they were never artificial. The year that he passed away was the first time I ever had an artificial tree. I placed it on my coffee table. The following Christmas I had that same 18 inch tree on the table.

This evening I'm remembering something that happened that second year that he was gone. It's a wonderful memory that I'm grateful to have. Here's what happened:

A few evenings before Christmas Molly started barking ferociously. (She barks at family as much as she barks at strangers.) I didn't immediately go to the door because I wasn't expecting anyone, and it was dark outside. The barking continued for a couple of minutes, and then I heard someone say, "Mom."

141

When I opened the door there were four big smiles standing in front of me, along with a beautiful live Christmas tree. Michael put it on a stand and put lights on it, and then the girls decorated it. Michael also put up lights on the outside of my house. Aaliya's sister, Aleysha, had brought homemade brownies, and I had eggnog in the fridge. My house looked and felt like Christmas.

I'll always be grateful how much their thoughtfulness brightened that Christmas season for me, and for the love that I felt.

December 21st

The news said that the Christmas Star hasn't been visible since 1623, and it won't be visible again until 2080. I wasn't here for the last one, and I probably won't be here for the next one.

I'm grateful that I got to see it tonight.

December 22nd

Today I'm grateful for a mistake that I made. I inadvertently called a friend that I had no plans to call. However, that call turned out to be to the right person, at the right time, and it helped to allay a worry that I had.

I'm grateful that I accidentally called Nancy.

December 23rd

I know that Christmas Eve isn't until tomorrow, but throughout the day today I kept thinking of the best Christmas Eve I ever had.

I had been in the hospital for more than a month due to complications from my cancer treatment. It was through the grace of God, help from many doctors, and Dave's tenacity in staying on top of the doctors that pulled me back from the brink of death.

After we had driven home from the hospital late on that Christmas Eve night, Dave parked the car in the driveway, got out of the driver's seat, and ran around to open my door. He helped me to get out of the car and walked slowly with me towards the front door. My hands were holding on to the handles of a walker. Dave lovingly had his arm around my waist.

The first thing I saw when I walked through the doorway was a beautifully decorated Christmas tree and four stockings hanging by the fireplace. For weeks I wasn't sure if that was something I would ever see again. My closest friends and family had those same thoughts.

Even though I had lost a lot of weight, and all of my hair, and it was difficult to walk, and for the first time in decades I wouldn't be attending Midnight Mass, it didn't matter. I had received the best gift in the world–I would be waking up on Christmas morning in my own home with Dave, Michael, and Kathleen all there with me.

I was and I am grateful and blessed.

December 24th

This Christmas Eve is only the second time in many years that I didn't attend Midnight Mass. My church had a Midnight Mass, but due to COVID- 19 I didn't feel comfortable going to it.

However, I did feel comfortable attending the 4 p.m. outdoor Mass where each family was socially distanced from other families. There were boxes drawn on the grass with chalk, and each family stayed within their box. Kathleen, Aaliya, Faz, and I sat in a chalked off box on chairs that we each had brought from home. Michael couldn't join us because he had to work. Our friends, Gail and Joe, were in the marked box next to us.

I'm grateful that I had the opportunity to attend this beautiful Mass with my family and friends, and to receive Communion for the first time since March.

December 25th

When I was driving home from yesterday's Mass my brake and my ABS indicator lights came on. The speedometer needle had also stopped working and stayed on zero.

Michael and Aaliya were hosting Christmas at their home today, but I didn't feel safe driving my car.

I'm grateful that Michael picked me up and brought me to his house. It was a wonderful day and I'm blessed that I was able to spend it with my family. I think we may have started a new tradition because after dinner we once again played Bananagrams.

I'm grateful that at the end of the day Aaliya's dad, Faz, and her sister, Aleysha, drove me home.

December 26th

I spoke with my cousin, Maureen, today. It's been eight years since we've seen each other, but whenever we speak on the phone it's like we've never been apart.

Maureen is another one of my cousins who was born in Ireland but who lived with my parents and me after arriving in America as a teenager. I have many fond memories of her from when I was a child, but one that still makes me smile was when I was about four years old and she was teaching me how to do the Irish jig.

Today I'm grateful for happy childhood memories with Maureen.

December 27th

I'm grateful that when I was taking the groceries out of the backseat of my car, the wasp that flew into my car quickly flew out again.

December 28th

I am so grateful for the scrumptious dinner that I had tonight. Faz and Aleysha planned and treated the family to dinner at a tapas restaurant. The food kept coming throughout the evening, and it was absolutely delicious! I seriously don't remember when I've eaten so much.

As wonderful as the food tasted, enjoying it with my family was the best part of the evening.

December 29th

Joey is the person whom we call when a hurricane or a windstorm has damaged screen panels on our pool's screen enclosure. We haven't needed his help for a few years, but recently high winds tore out one of the large screens over the pool. This opening seemed to be an invitation for birds to fly into my patio area, but then they couldn't figure out how to get out for several hours.

Today Joey replaced the screen. He also cleaned out the leaves in the gutters, as well as the plants that were growing in the gutters.

I'm grateful for Joey, and I appreciate all the work he does for me.

December 30th

I had to go to the bank today to get a cashier's check. I'm grateful that Jessica didn't charge the $10.00 service charge.

December 31st

Today is the last day of 2020. I'm glad that it's coming to an end, and I pray that 2021 will be a better year for us all.

Tonight when there were only a few hours left in 2020, I stood alone on my pool deck and stared at the full moon that was reflecting on the lake. It was spectacular!

I'm not sure if gazing at this stunning sight was a good way to say "Goodbye" to 2020, or if it was a good way to welcome 2021. Maybe it was a little bit of both.

I'm sincerely grateful to have seen this beautiful view tonight. I'm grateful for all my blessings in 2020.

Afterword

I hope that you enjoyed reading Grateful and Blessed. I certainly enjoyed writing it, and being reminded of the many things I had to be grateful for during 2020. Had I not put pen to paper at the end of each day, and jotted down notes of the things that had blessed me, I would have only remembered a fraction of those blessings.

Most days I was grateful for something that happened that particular day.

Other days, memories of happy times from the past often brought a smile to my face, and gratitude to my heart. Little did I know when we were making those memories that one day I would be thinking about those moments in time, and that they would be a source of happiness for me during a pandemic.

I think that most of us would agree that 2020 was a year like no other. But as unpleasant as it was, I could still easily find at least one reason each day that caused me to be grateful. Had I not kept a daily gratitude journal, however, I'm quite sure that I'd be looking back at 2020 as a year of darkness. Now, when I read my journal I see rays of sunshine in my life every day.

I was hopeful that 2021 would be a better year for us all. But, we don't always get what we hope for. Shortly after we left 2020 behind us, I was diagnosed with COVID- 19. My diagnosis came the day before I was to get my first vaccine.

I didn't feel well, and being in quarantine was more difficult for me than the lockdown had been. But, just like 2020, 2021 has given me much to be grateful for.

My doctor was awesome, and I think he helped to make my COVID- 19 experience easier than what it could have been. As important as my doctor was to my recovery, however, my family and friends were just as important, and they were with me every step of the way.

When they learned of my diagnosis, they immediately went to the pharmacy and brought me what the doctor said I needed to take. While I was in quarantine they left groceries on my front porch. They also delivered homemade meals, delicious soups, and takeout meals. Not having to cook for myself for weeks was appreciated more than words can say. The food that my friends and family provided me nourished my body. The calls, and texts, and email, and cards they sent me lifted my spirits, and nourished me emotionally.

I'm glad that I started writing in my journal before the pandemic began, and that each day there was something to be grateful for. Thanks to my journal I can see that gratitude continued to be my attitude, even during the pandemic.

I hope that after reading my book, you'll consider keeping a gratitude journal. Try it for a while. See what you think. Do it by yourself, or do it as a family around the supper table. I'd venture to say that each day you will find something that made you smile, or helped you in some way.

I know that life still isn't back to normal, but I strongly believe that we're getting closer to the day when we'll be able to breathe a huge sigh of relief, and that we'll be back to normal once again.

Here's to normalcy and to gratitude!

Acknowledgements
Part Two

Most book authors have an Acknowledgements page to thank the people who helped them with their book. I'm no different. What is different is that I'd like to give a more detailed acknowledgement of someone. That someone is Kathleen. Here's the reason why...

A few times in my book I alluded to not being tech savvy. That's probably an understatement.

When I wrote my first book, I used a word processing software which is how authors write their books. However, I had a problem with it–lines, paragraphs, and pages of text disappeared before my eyes. Thankfully, my computer wizard husband was able to resolve the problem.

Since I no longer have Dave to come running to my rescue, I knew that I had to do something different with this book. My solution probably isn't one that other authors would have chosen, but it worked for me. And, it helped me focus on the words that I was writing, rather than being worried about deleting my book.

The unconventional answer to my problem was that I wrote the entire book in email.

Kathleen took what I sent to her and put it all in Word, and later sent it to John. She said that it was easy to do, but in my humble opinion "easy" is in the eye of the beholder.

Without her help, I sincerely don't think this book would have come to fruition.

I'm grateful for her help, and I'm blessed that she's my daughter.

CPSIA information can be obtained
at www.ICGtesting.com
Printed in the USA
BVHW031410280422
635622BV00007B/284